EVERYDAY
MONEY

EVERYDAY MONEY

How to Manage Your Money
the Smart and Easy Way

JULIE FENSTER

A BYRON PREISS BOOK

Doubleday Direct, Inc.
Garden City, New York

CONTENTS

Dedicated to my mother and father

INTRODUCTION

If you are anything like the average reader of *EveryDay Money*, you're really not so bad with personal finances. Your checkbook ledger is as neat as a pin *(it doesn't have anything written in it)*. Your retirement is perfectly planned *(nobody can lose forty-five years' worth of lotteries)*. And just as rock solid is your health policy *(always put broccoli on everything)* and your disciplined savings *(of frequent-flyer miles)*. If you actually are anything like the average reader of *EveryDay Money*, you are as smart as a whip in something, or many things, but matters of personal finance have so far failed to sink in. Where can you begin to catch up?

Here. *EveryDay Money* is where you can relax about personal finance. This is a different kind of book, where you have fun and make fun, but you also come to recognize personal finance as *your* finance.

EveryDay Money was written to make sure that you understand all the major tools at your command in money management so that you will feel at ease with terms and trends. You can have confidence in your decisions and control your part of any conversation about your money. There will be no more peculiar silence from your corner when people speak to you about time deposits, mutual funds, pensions, policies, or planning. We have given the changing world of personal finance some perspective: You are in the midst of an important revolution. Where individual money management is concerned, you have new responsibilities. You're not sure you want them? Don't bother thinking about it; you have them.

EveryDay Money isn't always in a nice mood. Some of the things that go on with money have to make you mad. But unlike some books so well presented on personal finance, this one wants to have a good time, most of the time. If even one person puts down a steamy French novel to finish *EveryDay Money,* then the book will have been a success. If even one person learns from it how to use money to take control of the future, then that reader will be the success. That would make the author far happier yet.

EVERYDAY
MONEY

Chapter 1

SAVINGS AT THE START

YOU MUST REMEMBER THIS

Personal finance has grown more complicated in the past few generations as the power of money has shifted to people of all incomes. As the options have multiplied, the obligation to understand them has intensified. Unlike in previous generations, each person today is responsible for her or his own financial future. . . . In building assets, a balanced portfolio is even more important than the size of an overall fortune. Among the major types of assets to build and coordinate are bank and savings accounts; real property; Wall Street investments; pensions and retirement accounts; and life insurance. . . . Banking accounts are the most basic of all assets and can accelerate or drain savings, depending on how they are used. The U.S. Treasury offers the safest choices in long-term savings for any amount from $25 to $100,000.

MONEY EQUALS POWER

The Du Ponts came to this country from France in 1800 with quite a lot of money and farseeing thoughts about the future. Their plan, kept secret on the voyage, was to colonize Virginia. On arrival, though, they were rudely informed that Virginia was already a state and didn't wish to be colonized—a fact that made the Du Ponts dejected and depressed. But not for long, because they had enough money to be flexible, so they started a chemical factory instead.

For most people throughout history, money was an absolute. It bought umbrellas; that was its purpose. Only the rich, like the Du Ponts, knew the extra dimension of money: that a person could use it to exert control over the future.

Money by itself equaled bread or bricks.
Money plus time equaled power.
Money plus time plus discretion equaled destiny.

Knowledgeable people with the money to invest for a span of years could actually affect the future, as it applied to them. It was the greatest of privileges. Meanwhile, just about all that people of the lower or middle classes could do was work hard, save money, and hope for the best. In the United States up to the earlier years of the twentieth century, small investors had few options, except to save their money in simple ways. Zipping it into a purse was not really much different from putting it into a bank account. While purses did indeed disappear without a trace, so did banks in those days.

More recently, though, the very power of money has become more accessible to the general populace. Over the course of the last century, owners of banks, brokerage houses, and credit companies discovered that they could become billionaires by helping would-be millionaires. Investment advisers formerly engaged by a few rich families became mutual fund managers, dispensing the same expertise to anyone who came along with the price of a share. The result is a whole generation of mini-tycoons. For nearly everyone today, money is two entities under one name (just as it always has been for the wealthy). Money is *moola,* the value of a can of paint or an hour of your time. And money is also a way of controlling your destiny, a whole system of money–plus-time–plus discretion that lets you make long-term plans and then keep them. One of the accomplishments of our age is that people with just $1,000 can combine it with time and a decision in order to see into their own future.

A good many people with money of their own can't quite sort out all that is going on in personal finance. But ignorance isn't really much of an option, anymore. The relatively recent freedom to manage even a small nest egg like a big-time tycoon has turned into an obligation to do nothing less.

MONEY ETIQUETTE

Never brag about your money, or your way with it, and don't be intimidated by those who do.

Know without exception that the dollar you owe a friend is worth exactly the same as the dollar a friend owes you.

Never say you're poor; it's a bore.

Always interrupt when you don't understand something a financial professional says. Don't waste time pretending.

And, most important, always be proud that you have your financial home in good order, and that you had the biggest part in building it.

MAPPING YOUR MONEY

Have you ever, on a dark and stormy night with nothing much to do, taken your savings bonds out of the envelope in the cigar box at the back of the drawer, and spread them out on the bed? Perhaps you made a little train track of them — counting them, adding up the face values, shuffling them, and fluttering them like a deck of cards. Then you stacked them neatly back in the drawer for the next time a storm keeps you in. Nothing has quite the glow of assets, but not all of them are as easy as bonds to play with — or even to see at a glance. In your mind, develop a well-lit display, a veritable topography, of all your assets so that you can see them clearly, along with any liabilities you may have.

Worldly Goods

In personal finance, assets are as immediate as the nickels rolling around in your raincoat pocket and as distant as a retirement account that cannot be disturbed for fifty years. Toting up the overall amount doesn't matter as much as understanding the composition. The safety isn't in the numbers, anyway, but in having an unbroken ring of assets around yourself and your family. Safe bets are

Banking and savings vehicles: Short-term savings or checking accounts are daily staging areas, whereas long-term savings instruments ought to represent one year's household income, in case of emergency. (An instrument would be, for example, a Treasury bill, a money market fund, or a CD, all of which are described in this chapter.)

Life insurance policies: These are not necessary for everyone but are vital for the head(s) of any family.

Real property: This includes anything you can bump into—a house, a car, a big diamond ring.

Retirement plans: Started in conjunction with an employer or the government, pensions build up through the years and may not be worth anything immediately. Private retirement accounts are full-fledged assets from the start.

Investment portfolios: These contain a variety of stocks, mutual funds, bonds, and other instruments.

Business assets: An asset in the form of a privately owned business can easily change the priorities regarding other personal assets. Entrepreneurs typically neglect all the categories above in favor of pouring every red cent into a business. They shouldn't, since there is really no such thing as short-term planning in a well-run business or career. But they will, believing that a growing business is life insurance, real estate, retirement savings, and investment all rolled into one. Just the same, if you own a business, cultivate your other assets as though you don't.

A strong ring of assets is composed of at least four of the categories, with the added strength of variety within each.

The Minus Pool

(This part is not nearly as much fun as Worldly Goods.)

When considering your current assets, as outlined above, cast a colder eye and make the following adjustments:

• Deduct outstanding personal loans and credit card balances from your banking accounts. Loans of any type are liabilities—obligations that must be met by your assets.

• Property listed under real estate isn't worth what you paid for it, but rather what it can bring. In the case of a home with a falling price and a mortgage, you could well lose money. In the case of a new car with a lot of financing, you definitely would. Decisions regarding real property are not often made on a purely financial basis, and so they are compromised as assets. Yet the worth of your home, automobile, jewelry, and other valuables—the *assessed* value—is important because it could affect decisions regarding other assets.

The Primordial Soup

Liquidity refers to the ease with which you can turn your assets into cash, ready to spend on anything you like. Most real estate is not liquid; it takes months to sell buildings or property. It usually takes weeks to find a fair price for jewelry and collectibles. Stocks could be liquid (transactions on most markets clear in three days) except for one problem: If you sell in a hurry, you might have to sell at a loss. In terms of liquidity, your assets should range from the rocky to the mushy to the downright watery.

Examples of *very liquid* assets: checking and savings accounts; cash; mature U.S. savings bonds; traveler's checks; . . . and returnable empty bottles.

Examples of *quite liquid* assets, with which you may suffer a penalty or loss for early redemption but can at least have your money within about three days: mutual funds; stocks; CDs; U.S. savings bonds only a few years old; . . . and returnable bottles that are still full and have to be opened and emptied.

Examples of *not very liquid* assets, with which you will suffer a penalty for early withdrawal and also wait for several weeks for your money: retirement accounts; life insurance policies; . . . and returnable bottles that you got while on vacation in another state and have to actually mail back to redeem.

Examples of *non-liquid* assets, which will require great amounts of time, effort, or luck to turn into cash: equity built into homes; buildings; land; automobiles; jewelry; collectibles; . . . and nonreturnable bottles.

Air Is Not Liquid

Credit is so widely available today that many people are reducing their liquidity, assuming that should any need for spending power arise, they will be able to handle it through their credit cards or a bank loan. Many employers will also make retirement savings accounts available for a good cause. Nonetheless, a basic facet of financial security is independence, and a person should aim to have about one year's after-tax income in very liquid or quite liquid assets, as described above. That amount will also save you money through the years by allowing for a degree of self-insurance or high deductibles in many of the policies you take out. Since catastrophes occur not only to individuals but also to institutions, to regions, and, in economic terms, to whole countries, some of these particular assets should not be subject to fluctuation and should be fully insured, such as fixed-rate CDs or U.S. Treasury obligations.

THE BIG WALLET:
BANKING INSTITUTIONS

Believe it or not, banks used to have personality. A little. Throughout the first seventy years of the twentieth century, commercial banks were lean and mean, catering to businesses. Savings banks (both the savings and loan associations and the mutual savings banks) were the good guys, issuing home mortgages to help their neighbors. Even their nickname, "thrifts," sprang from a certain admiration for the character trait that they encouraged in others. James Stewart played a banker, distinctly an S&L banker, in *It's a Wonderful Life.* Had he been a commercial banker, he would not have had such sentimental ties to Bedford Falls; he would have been long gone at the beginning of the movie, off to adventure, and they would have had to change the title to *Casablanca.*

Banks have grown more alike since the 1980s, squeezed into one another's yards by increased competition and decreased regulations. First, commercial banks began to be more friendly toward the rabble, offering an array of small-time accounts and loans aimed at individuals. On the other side of the ever-lowering fence, the government gave thrifts the right to make business loans—a right that some of them abused without delay by slipping loans to their buddies. The loans had absurdly low interest rates, secured with practically nonexistent collateral. The S&Ls in question—a small percentage of the entire group—didn't reserve enough cash in their own accounts to cover bad loans. Bad loans? Would their friends ever, in a million years, let them down? You ought to know the answer, considering that it cost your household and every other one in the country $800 to bail out, or balance the ravaged books of, the couple of hundred worst S&L cases. In the aftermath, regulations regarding loans and reserves were tightened.

The lesson for the rest of us ought to be that while banks are the pillars of our way of life, they are also, to purposely mix metaphors, little kids who have to be watched. And the more they say they don't have to be watched, the more they *do* have to be watched.

Commercial banks and thrifts may scrap among themselves, but they face their greatest competition today from outside the realm. Brokerages, credit card companies, and insurance companies now offer banking services and resemble banking institutions in that respect. The signal difference is that *only banks* are required to insure accounts.

Another type of banking institution is the credit union, that little building on the side street. If you belong to one, you know it is a nonprofit organization with limited services and good rates for employee and civic groups. If you don't belong to one, you will wonder how anyone can possibly put money into a banking-type institution that doesn't even have a jingle on the radio. In the first place, credit unions don't have to advertise because membership is usually closed to outsiders. In the second place, they are by nature very quiet.

The credit union was invented in Germany in the mid-1800's to afford credit to working-class people who couldn't hope to receive it from banks. Such people wanted home-loans, even though their only collateral was, literally, an honest face. Spreading to the United States and Canada in the 1920's, the credit union evolved into a super-duper thrift, owned and operated by people who trusted each other on the basis of some shared sense of future—people working for the same company or within the same industry, for example. Normally, a credit union can offer advantageous interest rates on both deposits and loans, due to the low margin extracted to cover overhead.

Thankin' Franklin

After such antiheroes as Butch Cassidy and the Sundance Kid or Jesse James robbed a small bank—which was the favored type for robbing—depositors were antirich, which is to say, their money was gone. The bank passed the loss along. Even without help from a desperado, banks quite often would collapse, falling in on bad loans or bad management; then, too, the depositors were wiped out. Every so often, the news that someone had defaulted on a big loan would start the rumor that the bank was going to collapse. The depositors would descend on the bank, remove all their money, and so make absolutely certain that it did collapse.

The Great Depression exacerbated banks' problems, and rampant collapses forced President Franklin Roosevelt to close all banks for a month in 1933. His administration recognized that it could not rebuild the economy on such quicksand. It introduced strict new bank regulations and also started forcing banks to buy insurance on nearly all accounts. Banks still collapse from time to time, but debts are never passed on to depositors.

Each depositor at a bank or a thrift is insured for up to $100,000, through the Federal Deposit Insurance Corporation. That figure may be higher if more than one person is named on the account. If and when you pass the insured amount, start a new account at another bank. Credit unions are not required to insure deposits, though the government offers NCUIF (National Credit Union Insurance Fund) insurance, and you will want to be sure that your own accounts are so covered. You can also purchase private insurance on certain instruments or accounts serviced through a brokerage.

Choosing a Bank

As you probably know, banking institutions make money by accepting deposits at 5 percent and loaning it at 10 percent, or numbers like that. It is an unusual business, buying and selling the use of money. More and more, however, banks are making huge profits in much the same way dry cleaners do—by charging for services: two dollars here, four dollars there, ten dollars for this, and a buck a month for that. It seems needless to finish the paragraph by saying that many customers are being taken . . . to the cleaners.

In deciding where to open an account, you have to balance a list of probable fees against any interest that is offered. Looking past the prevailing interest rate that first catches your eye, here are some other considerations when choosing a bank:

1. **Settle in for the long haul.** A stable banking history counts in your favor if you apply for a loan, especially from the same bank. Books used to recommend that you establish a cordial relationship with your banker, chatting

with him or her about football scores and last year's vacation. Not to be cynical, but that may be too much to ask in our day, when tellers would proof Ulysses S. Grant if he came in and asked for change of a fifty. Do your best. And don't always use the automatic teller machine (ATM); it won't put in a good word for you when you need it most.

2. Ways and means. Your accounts have to fit your frame of mind: Banks do or don't return checks with statements; they will or won't issue passbook accounts; they can or cannot accommodate online banking; they may or may not charge for teller service. Location counts for a lot, too, and a distant bank may well discourage good habits. You may, for example, quietly pile up a fortune in charges for using offsite ATMs.

3. Minimum balances. It will probably occur to you that free checking isn't free if you have to keep a lot of money in a non–interest-bearing account in order to qualify. What is the humblest annual interest on a typical minimum of $5,000—about $200? That is how much free checking will cost you under such circumstances. Some banks will count all your various accounts toward meeting minimum requirements.

Banks in Our Time

In the days before NOW (negotiable orders of withdrawal), about 1970 and earlier, savings accounts at various banks paid out a narrowly competitive interest rate, while checking accounts cost customers money. The savings account was the simpler, since withdrawals had to be made through the bank, then as now. The checking account, however, was sophisticated stuff because it allowed third parties to make withdrawals on the basis of the signed authorization known originally as a draft and later as a check. Money didn't slide across tables; it fluttered through the air.

At the beginning of the 1970s, brokerage houses created money market fund accounts that paid interest rates high enough to make savings accounts look sickly. The sound of money bobsledding into brokerages in the mid-1970s woke up the banks, which demanded new regulations giving them the right to offer a type of interest-bearing checking account, in direct competition with money market accounts. The result was NOW checking.

Checking accounts. Most banks offer both regular checking and NOW checking. A regular type of account is likely to charge a fee but offer unlimited check-writing privileges. While it probably won't pay interest on your balance, a NOW account will. Somewhat of a cross between savings and checking, a NOW account is likely to have a steep minimum balance.

You might never even write a check and yet have a mighty active checking account. The most popular use of the ATM is, in effect, cashing a check or making a personal withdrawal. Except under special circumstances—for example, depositing your winnings in Las Vegas just before having the chance to lose them—you should refrain from using an ATM for deposits because the receipt will not carry any legal weight in the event of a dispute. The fees associated with the use of ATMs have become scandalous. The best way to avoid unnecessary charges is to know what they are; you'll soon figure out a way to avoid them (changing banks, for instance; withdrawing more than eight dollars at a time, for instance; establishing, for instance, check-cashing privileges at a convenient grocery store).

The *debit card*, often issued as an ATM card, is a plastic version of a check, but it has a sharper edge — truly. If you use a debit card to make a purchase at a store, funds are transferred electronically from your account to that of the store . . . instantly. A paper check might sit in a cash register long enough for you to run to the bank and cover it with a quick deposit. Not a debit card, though. Guard your debit card. To a thief, it is equivalent to cash on the barrelhead, and as far as your bank is concerned, it was (note *was*) your money, not the bank's. Depending on your bank, though, the loss will be limited if you report the missing card immediately.

By an arrangement called *automatic deductions*, you can authorize the bank to make certain monthly payments, usually in satisfaction of car or home loans wherein the amounts never vary. Some creditors lower interest rates for customers who agree to automatic deductions.

Finally, in this roster of noncheck checking, you can sit at your computer and pay bills by means of online banking. This service has been available through telephone modems since the early 1980s, though customers didn't rush to embrace it until it went on the Internet.

The majority of the nation's larger banks now offer full online services, while a growing number of institutions have recently been chartered specifically for the Internet. As with other areas of E-commerce, overhead costs are substantially lower for such banks, so customers have been able to find more favorable rates of interest on both sides of their transactions: in opening accounts or in taking out loans. Many people are receiving as well as paying their bills in the same paperless way, which is another factor that may lead to reduced costs for you. Security is high in all legitimate online banks, but the comfort level will never be high enough for many people, who like to be able to criticize their "*&%#! faceless bank" directly to its face.

Savings accounts. As for savings, practically everything and anything is a savings account now. Most banks will offer several variations, including a dedicated savings account with slightly higher interest than the NOW account. Few banks still offer a passbook account, though it has the advantage of straightforward recordkeeping and tradition, both of which encourage some people to make it grow, page by page. Special accounts, such as Christmas Clubs and Vacation Clubs, are installment savings plans in which the interest rate is almost invariably low, compared with other savings accounts. They may, however, get the job done for some people. Whatever account suits you, look to see how often the interest is *compounded,* or how often the interest is added to your account so that new interest can be paid on the old. The more often, the better for the account holder.

When your savings account reaches about $5,000, you should begin to think about transferring funds into one of the long-term savings vehicles described in the next section.

CHECKS AND BALANCES

You undoubtedly knew what a checkbook account was, even without reading this book. It's a modern invention for scaring adults.

The "I Can't Do Checking" Encounter Group

"It's like, I don't know. Things are disappearing, you know," says the fashionable-looking woman with the sunglasses. "I don't know—I really don't—where on *earth* I've written the checks. I wrack my brains, but I can't remember. I can't write it down on that thing that comes with the checkbook, because I'm always in a rush. Anybody who knows me knows that."

(Should we buzz through and tell her to get a duplicate checkbook that makes a carbon copy of the check while she's writing it? The cost is about double that of regular checks.)

"It doesn't matter if you write it in granite," adds the man with the yellow vest. "There is no such thing as *time* with a statement. By the time the statement comes, it's missing some of the checks I already wrote. How am I supposed to balance something that's never completely up-to-date?"

(It's really tempting to buzz. He would be an excellent candidate for an online account so that he can monitor his account activity. He should still check over his monthly statement, though, since it is the legal record of his account.)

"Once"—it's the woman who never looks up—"I put a certified check in my account for . . . for $8,600. Then I wrote a check for $4.70 to my library to cover overdue fines. It bounced. With more than eight thousand dollars in the account, the bank bounced my check to the library."

(Banks are legally obligated to recognize funds from checks on a schedule ranging from one to five business days. Crisscrosses go in their favor. We should really buzz in and tell the woman who never looks up, however, that some banks have a policy of looking at account activity before returning a check. If a deposit of any kind is pending, they will give the account holder the benefit of the doubt and stave off the bounce. What's that noise? Good grief, somebody is buzzing us.)

("Uh, yeah. We're watching you right now from the other side of *the mirror, the one by the door. We've been watching you watch the encounter group. You might want to mention that the woman who never looks up should also arrange for overdraft protection with her bank. That's an automatic loan that kicks in whenever her checking account can't cover a check.")*

(Let's get out of here. If you have to, you can come back next week and join the encounter group yourself. Payment by cash only.)

LONG-TERM SAVINGS VEHICLES

VIVs

We won't give a glib subtitle to this section, because it is a strictly formal affair. It's about VIVs (Very Important Vehicles). If you haven't met these types before, you are going to be introduced now.

Certificates of Deposit (CDs). When you put money into a regular savings account, you need not tell the bank when you're going to take it out. You can surprise them and take it out right after they've loaned it to someone else. (You pixie.) Across the board, a certain percentage of depositors do that day after day so banks have to reserve about 15 percent of all deposits—keeping it on hand as dead weight—in case depositors want it.

The CD is a special note through which you promise to leave between $500 and $100,000 in a bank for a set amount of time, ranging from seven days up to ten years. The interest is higher than it is in a savings account because the bank can plan on using all of the money the whole time. Rates can vary even at a single bank, running higher for more money on deposit for longer periods.

Profile: CDs can be purchased through banks or stock-brokers. Those purchased at banks are fully insured, but they can't be cashed without a stiff penalty on the interest. CDs issued by brokerage houses are not insured per se, though they often represent underlying bank-issued CDs that are. Brokerage-house CDs can easily be cashed prematurely.

Tip: Variable Rate versus Fixed Rate—CD interest rates move steadily with the nation's overall rates, which are indicated by Treasury bonds. Usually CDs only move a little, but sometimes a lot. What if you buy a long-term CD at a fixed rate of 5 percent, and before it is halfway to maturity you see that the current rate is 8 percent? Congratulations! Now you're an investor. However, you may be able to cash the CD at a penalty of some interest, and then buy into a better rate that will make up the loss. Or you can purchase a variable rate CD to begin with, riding the rates up and down.

Tip: Effective Annual Yield—Compounded interest is the secret friend of many an old fortune in this country, and it makes a difference in what are known as true rates for CDs. Advertisements for CDs display two numbers, as in 8.2/8.77. The first is the actual rate of annual interest, whereas the second, the effective annual yield rate, includes the influence that compounding brings to bear, to let you know exactly what percentage you can expect on a fixed-rate CD after one year. That figure, the true rate, is not as important to a CD with a term of only a few weeks or months; in that case, look more closely at the first number, the basic annual percentage rate.

Tip: National Sources — You need not live near the bank at which you have a CD, although you may well feel better knowing that you can go in and glare at someone in person should you have any problems. A full-service financial newspaper or an online service will list banks across the country offering the highest CD rates. You can call them yourself or enlist a local stockbroker to help make the long-distance purchase.

Shopper's Checklist: When you look around for a certificate of deposit, compare these characteristics:

1. Effective annual yield at one or two terms (lengths) of deposit acceptable to you;
2. penalties for early withdrawal;
3. financial condition of the bank, especially if the rate is notably high.

Money Markets. If a $100,000 certificate of deposit you couldn't afford paid a lot more interest than the $1,000 CD you *could* afford, there would be two ways to proceed. You could either sit down on the back porch feeling little and poor, or you could get your ninety-nine best friends together at $1,000 each and buy the better CD in a pool. Everybody would get the better interest rate. And that is the idea behind a money market fund, a type of account offered by brokerage houses.

"Money market" is an amusing image. Just picture a town square full of tables piled with money, customers fingering it to see if it's ripe. That's exactly what is out there, in the abstract: a money market in which the government is always a good customer for a loan, issued as a Treasury bill; in which banks, too, are writing CDs;

and in which corporations take out short-term loans at the prevailing rates. They are all looking for good money, and in the sense that time matters to all of them, they certainly do finger it first to see when it will be ripe. The hitch is that these good customers don't have all day to buy a sawbuck here, a greenback there, and a C-note or two on the way out. They are "wholesaler customers," and the typical minimum over which they will trouble themselves is $100,000. By starting a money market account, though, you can toss small amounts into that wholesale market. There are two ways to make the toss: the money market fund and the money market deposit account.

Profile: A money market fund is offered by a brokerage; you are officially a shareholder in the fund, though your deposit will be treated as if it were a cash account. The house takes about a half percent as a fee and returns all the other interest to the shareholders. A brokerage money market fund is not insured but is generally considered a safe place for money. You can write personal checks against a money market fund, enjoying good interest as well as total liquidity. The similar *money market deposit account* is offered by a bank, which sets a rate that is likely to be lower than that offered by the brokerage fund. The bank, however, will insure your account.

Tip: Special Funds—The brokerage money market fund can be tailored to your tax needs or other inclinations, through variations of the basic theme. For example, a *government-only* money market fund is intrinsically safe because it is restricted to federally-backed securities. A *municipal* money market fund is limited to local government issues, the interest earnings from which are not subject to federal income tax.

Shopper's Checklist: When you look around for a money market fund or account, compare these characteristics:

1. minimum balance required;
2. number of checks that can be written per month;
3. if there is a minimum amount on each check (sometimes $500);
4. in the case of the bank, how often interest is compounded;
5. in the case of a brokerage fund, the average duration of the investments in the portfolio (by law it must be shorter than ninety days—the shorter, the safer) and the management fee retained by the brokerage (it certainly shouldn't be more than one percent, if that).

AN INSPIRING STORY

Let's create a person. First, the name. Nan Tucket has a familiar ring. Profession? She works in the office of a little factory. We don't *know* what the factory makes at the moment; she hasn't opened the door to the back yet. We don't even know what she does. So far she's just reading something. It's something interesting. A paystub! Don't look, don't look.

Can't help it. She makes $1,000 per week, after taxes and her contribution to her pension. She looks worried. But why fret? That's a lot of income. She fills out a deposit slip: $200 into her savings account, per usual.

The person at the next desk is none other than her sister, Martha. We know what her last name must be, without even looking at the nameplate on the desk. The intercom crackles, "Miss Vineyard, your broker is on the telephone." Nan's pen runs out of ink at that very moment. Meanwhile, Martha is talking to the broker. Then she hangs up.

"Thank you for getting me this job that pays exactly the same as yours," she says to Nan. "How much do you have, now that it has been one year—counting the money that we inherited?"

"I save $200 a week, which I have been adding to my $10,000 inheritance in the savings account. I have $20,930," Nan says. Gales of laughter ring out. It doesn't seem all that funny, but finally Martha speaks.

"I save the same as you, $200, and I started with the same $10,000 inheritance," she says, choking with glee, "but I put my savings in a money market fund, and I put the inheritance into a one-year CD at an effective compounded rate of 6.2 percent. I have $21,721."

So, which sister has better finances? Nan Tucket—because Martha Vineyard was fired by her sister as soon as we left the office. But actually, their example shows that laziness or complacency can cost you real money, $791 in the plausible, all-too-common example above. Just about the cost of a vacation on . . . Block Island.

Treasury Notes, Bills, and Bonds

Some politicians, comparing the U.S. government with a household, tell voters that just as a family should not run up debt, neither should a government. Other politicians, comparing the government with a business, say that if a corporation ever operated on a big debt, it would be out of business. A government is neither a household nor a company. National debt is one of the means by which governments control the **overall** economy. Some national debt is entirely healthy; albeit, trillions of dollars' worth is something more than a hiccup in the other direction.

The U.S. government borrows money constantly, and very actively, through Treasury bills, bonds, and notes. U.S. savings bonds are one special type of bond; STRIPS are another. But when people speak of "Treasuries," they mean short-term *bills*, longer-term *notes*, and longest-term *bonds*. The rates for all three are set by big-time bidders in regularly scheduled auctions; smaller fish have to accept the resulting rates.

Profile: Notes, bills, and bonds (called obligations as a group) are as safe as the future of our government in America. (Fife and drums, please.) They are very safe. You can buy them directly from one of the twenty-five Federal Reserve Banks in this country or for a fee (of about $25) from brokers and most banks. The interest is fixed at the time the obligation is issued, and so it shall remain for its entire term, three months to thirty years.

How to spend, for example, ten grand at the Treasury:

1. Buy one $10,000 Treasury bill. The minimum purchase price for a T-bill is $10,000, and the term can be thirteen, twenty-six, or fifty-two weeks. The kick of a T-bill is that you will receive all the interest immediately, in the form of a check from the government. If you bought a twelve-month bill paying the rate of 5.26 percent, you'd receive a check for $500 within days—and then get the full $10,000 back in the allotted twelve months. This arrangement offers the ultimate in compounding, because you can then take the $500 and invest it in, say, a twelve-month CD paying 8 percent a year. At the end of twelve months, you'd have—why you'd have a fortune: $10,540.

2. Buy two $5,000 Treasury notes. You choose the amount of time and money, and the government will send you the interest every six months. Notes carry guidelines: The minimum term is two years; the maximum, 10 years.

The minimum investment is $1,000 for notes written for at least four years, while notes written for shorter periods are sold in $5,000 increments.

3. Buy one $10,000 Treasury bond. T-bonds have terms ranging from ten to thirty years, and a minimum amount of just $1,000. They are for soothsayers and people who believe that rates are just about as high as they're going to get.

Tip: Resale Market—Since the various notes, bills, and bonds lock in a rate derived from regular Treasury auctions, you may find yourself with a half-matured note paying 5 percent when new ones are paying 10 percent. You can't jump ship and cash an obligation early. You can, however, sell it on the secondary market through your broker. Who would want your paltry 5 percent obligation? Well, let's put it this way: Don't expect to get what you paid for it. Perhaps you'd receive $9,800. Just the same, you can find yourself holding a note paying 10 percent when the prevailing rate is 5 percent. Well, well, well—don't expect to *take* what you paid for it in that case. You might sell your obligation early for more like $10,200. (The figures quoted are only round numbers to make the point intended; major newspapers are neatly lined with the going prices on marketed Treasury bills, notes, and bonds.)

U.S. Savings Bonds

To begin with, savings bonds are patriotic. A good citizen buys bonds and thus lends money as a show of faith in the country. The livid citizen who picks up a pen to write a letter to the editor about the disgrace of the national debt might use the same pen to buy a few savings bonds. These bonds will do at least as much to stop the slide of money out of the U.S. Treasury, because the government doesn't have to pay as much interest to the holder of a savings bond as it pays to its other lenders. If, in a dream world, the entire national debt were financed by savings bonds, the annual deficit would be cut drastically.

Looking at savings bonds as a segment in the ring of assets that you are building around yourself, keep in mind that they are considered the very safest of all safe investments. They come in two forms: *Series EE* bonds pay interest tied to the average five-year Treasury rate; that may vary over the course of the bond. You get your money (and you can pay your taxes) when you cash the bond, and not before. A *Series HH* bond pays a rate of interest fixed at the time you purchase it. Your interest arrives every six months, nudging the deficit up by another trillion, or perhaps some fraction thereof.

Profile: The minimum investment for bonds is $25. They can't be cashed at all during the first six months, while incentives make it advisable to keep them at least five years, so they are not really liquid investments. Officially, Series HH bonds can only be purchased through branches of the Federal Reserve Bank, but banks that sell EEs can help obtain HHs. Interest on the bonds is subject only to federal income tax.

Tip: When to Take the EE Plunge —Buy your bonds on the last day of the month and you'll still get the whole month's interest. Bonds issued between 1973 and mid-1997 have a tricky accrual schedule. If they are more than nineteen months old, sell them either on the first day after the anniversary month or six months and a day after the anniversary month. Interest is only calculated every six months, so you could easily lose as much as a half year's interest with bad timing.

Tip: College Tuition—If you have a low- or middle-class income and are saving for a child's tuition, the interest on bonds is completely tax free. The IRS can supply you with the details of this admirable loophole (ask for Forms 8815 and 8818). Whatever you do, though, don't put the bonds in the name of your future baccalaureate. Put them in the name of the person on whom the child is officially dependent.

Zero-Coupon Bonds

In the olden days, a rich loafer was known as a "coupon clipper"—and not because he or she bought the Sunday paper in hopes of saving fifteen cents on pudding cups. Bonds are often issued with coupons on the side, and whenever interest is due, every six months usually, the holder cuts the dated coupon off to redeem it for cash in person or by mail. That method is not nearly as common today as it was fifty or a hundred years ago. Still, it exists.

What would happen, though, if the cat got hold of your bond and stripped the coupons off with his claws? And then ate them. Spit them up, maybe, but ruined them nonetheless. You would not get your interest money every six months, that is for sure. It would pile up with the actual value of the bond, and you'd get the whole amount when the bond matured—including interest on the piled-up interest. Thanks to the cat, you'd have much more money than if you'd taken your interest through the years and spent it on pudding cups.

The U.S. Treasury took that scenario and put it into practice with so-called zero-coupon bonds. They are issued already stripped of their coupons and their ability to distribute interest. That is why they are also called STRIPS, which is a tortured government acronym for Some Tabby Really Invented Patient Saving. It actually stands for Separate Trading of Registered Interest and Principal of Securities. STRIPS are excellent vehicles for long-term savings planned to the penny. You buy one for several thousand dollars today and in precisely twenty years, it will be worth precisely $20,000. The amount that you spend up front depends on the prevailing interest rate. Various amounts and terms are available.

Profile: You can buy the U.S. Treasury's STRIPS through a broker, the Federal Reserve Bank, or many other banks. They are as safe as any Treasury obligation. Banks and brokers can also sell zero-coupon bonds issued by private corporations and by brokerage houses, including Merrill Lynch and Salomon Brothers, which call their bonds TIGRs and CATS, respectively. The interest on zero-coupon bonds is taxable annually as it accrues; that is, you have to pay tax on money you won't see for years to come.

Tip: Retirement—If you buy a STRIP, or other zero-coupon bond, in a tax-deferred account such as an IRA, you will not have to pay income tax on the interest until you withdraw the money from the account.

HOW YOU WANT YOUR CHICKEN?

With the blues song, "How You Want Your Chicken," playing in the background, let's think about the low-risk investment vehicles discussed above and inquire . . .

How You Want Your Interest?	Look into a . . .
• All at the beginning	• Treasury bill
• Steadily, to live on	• Money market fund (brokerage) or money market account (bank); short-term CD
• Periodically, to reinvest	• Series HH savings bond; Treasury note or bond; long-term CD
• Not until the end of the term	• Series EE savings bond, zero-coupon bond

SELECTED GLOSSARY

Basis point: One-hundredth of one percent (0.01), a figure used in describing the movement of bond yields.

Certified check: A check covered immediately by a customer's account balance. When the customer presents a check for certification, the teller makes sure the account balance will cover it, withdraws the amount immediately to prevent the check from bouncing, and then stamps it. Nonetheless, many recipients demand the even more trustworthy **cashier's check,** by which a customer hands the teller money and receives a check drawn on the bank's own account.

Custodial account: An account opened by a customer in the name of a relative. The customer can make deposits, but no withdrawals, except along guidelines that protect the person in whose name the account was opened.

Rollover: A transfer of funds from one vehicle or account to another without disruption, especially in tax status.

Safe deposit box: A vault within the bank's own vault. The safe deposit box is essential for protecting legal documents, bonds, and valuables. The contents of the box are not insured by the bank. However, safe deposit insurance, offered by most insurance companies, will cover the contents both while they are in the box and when they are removed under normal circumstances.

Stop: A refusal by a banking institution, for a fee, to honor a check that you have written. As soon as possible, tell the person to whom you have written the check that it is no longer good. A stop can be used when a customer changes his or her mind, often after a high-pressure sales talk, or in cases wherein goods or services were not delivered as specified.

GET IN TOUCH

New York State Credit Union League
P.O. Box 15118
Albany, NY 12212
800–342–9835
To locate a suitable credit union anywhere in the country.

Federal Reserve System
20th St. and Constitution Ave., NW
Washington, DC 20551
202–452–3000
To find the closest branch to you, or to request a list of

the dozens of brochures on many subjects related to personal banking.

Treasury Department
U.S. Savings Bonds Division
1111 20th St., NW
Washington, DC 20226
304-480-6112 (customer service)
800-487-2663 (rate information)
Offers brochures, including a schedule of interest dates for all bonds issued.

Bureau of the Public Debt
1300 C St., SW
Washington, DC 20239
202-874-4000
Gives information on debt instruments issued by the federal government.

Veribank
P.O. Box 461
Wakefield, MA 01880
800–442–2657; fax, 781–246–5291
A private company that will send a detailed report on the financial standing of individual banks in the United States. Rates range from $10–$45, depending on the length of the report.

SIX FOR THE WEB

Good places to look for more information:

www.ibaa.org (Independent Community Bankers of America). Lists surcharge-free ATM machines by zipcode; carries banking news of interest to consumers, money management tips, and links to other sites.

www.aba.com (American Bankers Association). Offers an array of calculators, by which you can project mortgage payments, savings and college needs, auto payments, and the wisdom of buying versus renting.

www.bankrate.com (Bank Rate Monitor Infobank). Ranks account and loan rates at banking institutions all around the country.

www.sec.gov/oieal.htm (SEC's Office of Investor Education and Assistance). Provides timely tips about savings and investing, along with step-by-step advice on determining your goals and the vehicles available for obtaining them.

www.fdic.gov (Federal Deposit Insurance Corporation). Offers information on specific banks around the country; provides facts about banking insurance.

www.publicdebt.treas.gov (U.S. Treasury, Department of the Public Debt). Provides information and rates on Treasury bonds, bills, and notes, including the current worth of your savings bonds.

Chapter 2

TAKE CREDIT

YOU MUST REMEMBER THIS

Credit can either be secured by collateral, or be unsecured, as in the revolving credit offered through credit
cards. . . . Credit cards are easy to obtain and to use, but
they are probably the hardest aspect of personal finance
to control. Unnecessary interest charges and other fees
can tap money, while dependence on a credit card can
cripple a budget. A first step in selecting one is looking at
the disclosure chart included on every application. . . .
Everyone, even people who are married, should establish
an individual credit history that will help in obtaining a
loan whenever the need arises. . . . Among secured
loans, the home mortgage has so many variations that the
right one can have a deep impact on long-term planning
and can also make later refinancing unnecessary. . . .
Car leasing and car loans are more alike than different
from the consumer's point of view. Both can include
crafty hidden charges, but in the end, both should be
judged on the interest charged for the money used over a
certain period of time.

THE STREETS AREN'T PAVED WITH GOLD; THEY'RE COATED WITH PLASTIC

They don't give away money in our country, have you noticed? But they do give away credit. So even though our system will not give you any money, it will make you think of credit as money. Some people thus deluded fall hopelessly into debt, only to be left with neither credit nor money, neither reputation nor a sixteen-head stereo VCR.

Credit falls into two categories: secured and unsecured. Secured credit is backed by collateral and is normally under strict control. A home or car loan is secured by the home or the car. Unsecured credit, by contrast, is more nebulous. Bank cards, which represent by far the most prevalent type of unsecured credit, allow a cardholder to customize some aspects of a loan, simply by not repaying charges in full. A good customer might be required to pay back only $20 per month on a $1,500 balance. On that schedule, it would take almost five years to repay the $1,500 in principal—along with $2,750 in interest with a 19.6% annual percentage rate.

Well, that's absurd. Certainly it is. Not too astonishingly, bank card credit is now regarded as an addictive vice for some people, and with something of the same potential for self-destruction. Considering that this type of credit card account is only about a generation old, it has become a vital part of the working of the national economy, stoking sales and buffering the effects of recession. On the level of a personal economy, though, it is too easily misunderstood and can put an unnecessary drain on your money.

Using a credit card is like driving a tank. In both, it is

just as easy to veer off and cut a swath of destruction as it is to proceed straight down the road. For some people, staying in control is a cinch. Others never do figure out the controls—especially not forward and reverse. Eventually, they have to climb out, look back at what they have done to every store in town, and wait for someone to come and help clean up the mess.

But who was it who gave them the tank without giving them a lesson? How many advertisements made it evident that the working vehicle—that tank, that credit card—was a status symbol, available in gold or platinum? Who made it seem that customers get to go to Italy or Brazil on vacation if they have a credit card? Who designed the minimum payment to coax people into believing that they still have plenty of money left? People pay the minimum when all they have left is credit, and perhaps not much of it.

For all the licenses and all the credit cards in the average wallet (choking out the old movie stubs), there ought to be at least one more license: a permit to verify that the bearer truly understands credit cards.

The next section of this chapter is about credit and charge cards. Ten multiple choice questions are interspersed. Get a little piece of paper and write your answers down, letter by letter. If you answer all of them correctly, the letters will spell out a useful addition to your wallet.

Question #1: Credit cards are *not* any of the following, except
Q. a status symbol.
R. just the same as money.

S. a good way to take on a long-term loan.

T. convenient to use.

THE LAND BEFORE CREDIT CARDS

When you were little, did you wonder what people did before there were refrigerators, window screens, and credit cards? How could life be worth living? People way back in time may have had warm milk and bugs in the house, but they had a sense of community, and they certainly had credit, even without cards. Customers established an account at a particular store and did most of their shopping there. By the mid-1800s, some of the larger stores began to normalize such accounts, charging interest on outstanding balances. Department stores in New York started issuing little cardboard charge cards before World War I.

In the early 1950s, the modern era—our era—dawned when a New York advertising executive invented Diner's Club cards that would allow holders to charge meals at a variety of restaurants. And then hotels. And then American Express started its own card on an even grander scale in 1957. By the end of the 1960s, the Bank of America had helped launch a different type of card that gave extended credit to holders, and charged them interest for it. That led to Visa, MasterCard, and Discover cards.

Out of the short, lively history of credit cards developed two different strains: charge cards and credit cards, which include bank cards and store cards.

Charge cards allow customers to sign for purchases that must be paid for promptly (usually within sixty days). Interest is not charged, nor is extra time granted. Primary examples include American Express, Diners Club, and Carte Blanche.

Charge cards charge an annual fee ranging from $50 to $300. On the other side of the ledger, they also charge affiliated stores and restaurants up to 4 percent of each purchase. Businesses ante up because charge card customers have traditionally been big spenders, especially where travel and dining are concerned. They don't need extended credit; they do need convenience and the extra level of service associated with charge card billing and record-keeping.

What if you don't pay your balance on a charge card? First, you get a nice letter; then, a not especially nice telephone call; then, depending on your reputation, a harsh letter; finally, you receive a penalty fee of about $20 and can be charged interest on your balance.

Question #2: The charge card
A. does not exact any interest on your balance (unless it is vastly overdue).
B. repels mosquitoes.
C. changes color depending on your mood.
D. is worth minus-six in Hearts.

Bank cards and store cards allow customers *revolving credit* on their purchases. If customers pay for their purchases when billed, then the bank card is, for all intents and purposes, a charge card. (Bank card companies have been known to drop cardholders for doing such a thing.) The customer who doesn't pay the whole balance will be charged a minimum amount and interest on the remainder. That's all there is to it . . . except for the following:

1. **Grace Periods.** The card company may start charging interest against the amount of your purchase either the day you buy it or the day by which you were supposed to have paid your bill. That might be a difference of as much as two months, and it is known as the grace period. Some companies don't offer it at all, some always offer it, and some only offer it if you have no previous outstanding balance.

AN UNBALANCED COMPUTER

An engineer with a tiny balance of about $10 on her bank card bought a mail-order computer early one month. When the bill arrived, it already showed an interest charge of almost $50 on her big-ticket purchase. She screamed and hollered that she had had every intention of paying for it promptly, but the card company said that in view of the $10 outstanding balance, interest had kicked in the moment the computer purchase was made. The engineer finally paid the interest and destroyed the card in frustration.

Question #3: People who tend to carry balances should
M. not buy computers.
N. look for a card company that offers a grace period on all new purchases.
O. use backpacks.
P. keep their voices down.

2. **Annual percentage rate (APR).** The APR is otherwise known as the hole in the bottom of the bucket: the

smaller, the better. The rate can be fixed, but is often related to the prime lending rate, which is the interest rate the biggest banks in the country charge their best customers. A typical premium charged over that rate is 13.5 percent. To keep the high cost of convenience in perspective, consider that if the prime rate is 5.5 percent, then you might be able to get a personal loan from your bank at about 11 percent. These would both be secured loans. Meanwhile, you will pay 19 percent on your credit card balance—an unsecured loan.

Question #4: Manny has a $1,200 balance on his bank card at 18 percent. He will pay it off over the course of one year. On the other hand, he could take out a $1,200 secured loan against his car from the bank, at 12 percent interest, and repay the bank card company. Either way, he can afford to pay $100 per month. How much would Manny save by going to the bank for his loan?

J. 2,000 calories and 8 grams of fat.

K. about $50.

L. one touchdown.

M. five books of green stamps.

3. **Finance Charges.** The trouble with revolving credit is that it is dizzying, like going through a revolving door on roller skates. Well, sort of. You may be making charges against your credit card three times a day, changing the balance all the while. The card company has to choose a figure on which to charge your APR. Every night, while you are sleeping, they calculate what you

owe. (This is their favorite part of the day.) The figure
they come up with is based on the average of either the
current month's balance (known as the *average daily balance)* or the current and previous months' balances *(two-
cycle average daily balance)*. The former is preferable in
many cases. Either way, once they have a total, they add
$1/356$ of the current APR in interest. Then they go to sleep
and wait for you to wake up and go to the garden store
the next morning to buy planters. Even if you don't,
they'll still stay up late, just to reaverage your account
balance and add another $1/365$ of interest. And if you do
buy the planters, the card company may or may not start
charging you interest on their cost that very night. Look
past the APR itself to consider the method used for calculating the finance charge.

Question #5: Even if you paid off most of a big balance
last month (hurrah!), you may still be paying interest on
it. Why?
P. Because the card company uses the two-cycle method
of calculating the average daily balance and so the big
balance of last month is still part of the calculation this
month.
Q. Because you have a twin who looks exactly like Bette
Davis and she didn't pay off her balance last month.
R. Because the computer is down.
S. Because you didn't need planters in the first place.

Prime examples of bank cards are Visa, MasterCard,
Discover, Optima. Those are the family names. However,
the banks that issue the cards range widely in fee struc-

tures and service. With the exception of the American Express Optima card, the bank on your corner may issue your bank card, or a faceless bank in another state may do so. Some banking institutions are set up to do nothing but issue credit cards.

Adding to the swirl are special-issue bank cards connected with corporations, colleges, sports teams, and even charities. Either the cardholder or the contractor receives a kickback in money (or airline mileage points) on purchases charged to the card.

Look carefully at new credit card applications or at the back of your current bill. A disclosure chart something like the following will be readily obvious. Mandated by law, it is supposed to be a clear recitation of the terms that will most strongly affect the cost of credit to you. Our chart, below, will help to show you what to look for. The first column is standard; the second is copied exactly from an actual application. Normally, that is the extent of a disclosure chart, but we have added two more columns: one, to interpret the type of information given, and another to suggest ideas for you.

HOW TO READ A DISCLOSURE CHART

INFORMATION	ACTUAL SAMPLE	OTHER OPTIONS & NOTES	TIPS
Annual Percentage Rate (APR)	Sample: Variable 21.40% as of 4/8/00.	• Fixed or variable. • Date for sample should not be more than one year past; call for the current rate before applying.	Rate can be negotiable, depending on your credit history and spending patterns.

INFORMATION	ACTUAL SAMPLE	OTHER OPTIONS & NOTES	TIPS
Variable Rate Info	Your annual percentage rate may vary and is based on 13.5% above the highest U.S. prime rate as published in the *Wall Street Journal* Money Rates section. The annual percentage rate will not be less than 19.15%.	The rate is sometimes based on other standards.	Make sure to compare cards on the same standard, but look closest at the premium (amount above prime) used to determine the variable rate.
Grace Period for Purchases	If you pay your new balance in full by the due date shown on the statement covering the prior billing period (which is 25 days after the statement date), no finance charge is assessed in the current billing period.	Grace period can also cover all purchases, or no purchases. Chart writers are crafty coyotes.*	For those who carry a regular balance, a grace period covering all purchases can effectively cut the finance charge by a significant amount (a third in typical cases).
Balance Calculation Method	Two-cycle average daily balance (including new purchases).	• Average daily balance (one cycle) or two-cycle average daily balance. • Excludes or includes new purchases.	Order of preference for the average customer carrying a balance: 1. Average daily balance, 2. two-cycle. 1. Excludes new purchase, 2. includes new purchases.
Minimum Finance Charge	$ .50.	Can be more, but rarely is.	
Late Payment Fee	$15.	Should not be more than $20.	

*From another actual disclosure chart, this is the complete text of the grace period section: "20 to 25 days." That's all. It doesn't mention, except in the tiny print elsewhere, that that grace period of 20 to 25 days applies only *if you have no previous balance.*

HOW TO CHOOSE A BANK CARD

Part 1: The terms reflected in the disclosure chart will accurately show the effect of a card on your overall finances. **Part 2:** All things being equal, you can then choose a card that offers some perk—cash back or airline mileage, a sports logo on the face, an automatic donation to your favorite charity, even a low introductory APR. The Part 2 advantages rarely, if ever, make enough of a difference to influence any of the Part 1 considerations. Stick to the chart.

INTRODUCTORY INTEREST WON'T LAST: THE MUSICAL

The South Pacific: a clean, white boat, loaded with treasures and things like that, with a small passenger list of remarkably well-dressed people. Even the missionaries are well dressed. Ginny and Jack have fallen madly in love and leave the ship at Tonga, where they have dinner, the first meal for which they will have to pay. Ginny takes out a credit card and starts flipping it in her hand. Jack takes out his credit card, but barely glances at it.

"My dearest," he says to Ginny. "You pay for it. I thought this card had an APR of 5.6 percent, but I got my bill the other day and it's 19.6 percent now."

"You fool," Ginny retorts. "That 5.6 percent was the introductory annual percentage rate. That's no reason to get a credit card. You idiot. You didn't think it would last, did you?"

Jack looks at the tablecloth. "I always think it will," he admits. But when he looks up, Ginny is gone.

This harsh tale, loosely based on an opera by Puccini, must impress upon you the folly of ever jumping ship for the sake of an introductory interest rate.

Question #6: Which is *not* a valid reason to consider in a contract for a credit card?

B. The card has a variable rate tabulated at only 7 percent above the prime rate; most of the other cards you are considering have a rate tabulated at 10 percent or more above the prime.

C. The card offers a grace period on all purchases, whether you had a previous balance or not.

D. The card has no annual fee.

E. The card has a pretty picture on it.

Question #7: A customer receives a mailing that offers a Platinum Plus MasterCard, issued through a swanky New York store. The card features a 5.9 percent introductory rate, a $25 gift certificate at the store for every $2,500 charged on the card, and a $20 certificate just for being approved. What makes the card worth getting?

Q. Your friends might be impressed to see it in your wallet.

R. If you haven't had a walk through the disclosure chart and a look at the terms, you don't know anything about the card.

Credit Card Tips:

1. A charge card is a better beginner's card than a bank card. It demands discipline.

2. Your balance should be wiped clean at least once every three months.

3. No matter how many cards you have, if you are only paying the minimum . . .

    a. and you are carrying more than about $100 for

more than about three months, you will do well to take
money out of any liquid savings to clear your balance.

b. and your balance is more than about $1,000 for
more than three months, you will do well to look into
another type of loan from your bank to clear the balance.

c. and your balance grows to be more than one-twen-
tieth of your after-tax income, you must apply some discipline. (The simplest is to get rid of the card; however, just
leaving it at home most of the time may force you to begin
to pay cash, at least until you come out of the shadows.)

4. For personal finances, there is no reason to have
more than two bank cards or two charge cards. As to
store-issued credit cards, keep in mind that they distort
your best buying habits. The fewer you have, the more
free you will feel to comparison shop at a variety of
stores.

5. If you have a poor credit history or no credit history, many banks will arrange for a form of credit card
that is actually secured by a deposit. You will put, say,
$2,500 in an account that pays little or no interest and
have the use of a bank card with a credit limit of about
$2,000. If you don't pay your bills, the bank can dip into
the account. If you do pay your bills, you may well qualify for unsecured credit within a year or two.

6. If you can't pay your minimum, call the card company without delay and explain. The company will probably reduce the minimum if you will at least show good
faith and pay something. Remember that you are con-
tracted to the card company and want to keep them generally on your side if there is to be rough sledding.

Question #8: Aurelia has been carrying a $2,000 bank card balance for most of the year, at an APR of 19 percent. In August, she gets a $2,000 bonus check from her job. Her aunt, a well-known stockbroker, has given her tips on mutual funds, bonds, and several stocks poised for growth. What is the safest and most advantageous use for the bonus?

J. Buy a tax-free bond paying 6 percent.

K. Buy a mutual fund that Auntie says will probably grow at 10 to 12 percent this year.

L. Take a gamble on a stock that grew at 15 percent last year.

M. Pay off the bank card and take a personal gain of 19 percent.

Question #9: Sometimes clerks inadvertently enter a single charge two or even three times, in misreading confirmation codes from credit companies. What should you do to avoid paying for such mistakes?

H. Keep the receipts, but throw them on the floor of the car.

I. Keep receipts in an envelope and compare them with the statement when it arrives (then, if you like, you can throw them on the floor of the car).

Question #10: Credit cards are not the same as money. Except for those people who have a no-fee account and pay their monthly balance in full every time, the difference is that

T. dollar for dollar, credit cards always cost more to use than cash. (This varies, of course, with your habits, but if you do carry a balance, a rule of thumb is that a credit card dollar will cost you about $1.05.)

U. No other choices; reread T (above) about three times.

This ends the quizlet on your understanding of credit cards. If you passed, the card you made is now a "tank permit," and you can take the controls from here on out. If you didn't pass, no problem; there's an invention for you, too. It's called cash.

LENDERS BEWARE

The foregoing was meant to be a dour look at credit cards, a subject too often presented with all the sobriety of a roadside carnival. However, the world is a big place, full of sticky subjects. This brings us to a discussion of the only thing on earth that can make drowning in credit card debt look like a jolly pleasure. What could that be?

Loaning money to friends or relatives who are bad risks. Parents typically find themselves in the position of being the last resort for all those lost lambs to whom no one else will loan a nickel. No matter who is squeezing you for a loan, these two rules should apply at the very least:

1. Without saying it out loud, assume that you won't get the money back. If you really do need it back, then you just can't loan it on a personal basis. You may well lose both your money and your mind.

2. Write a memo relating the terms of the loan and the parties involved. You don't need a specific reason to do so. However, if any of the parties "go south" (or whatever

euphemism you use for dying), the estate must have a written record of the loan for tax and probate reasons. Don't neglect this, even if you have no intention of going south in the near future.

In the cold light of day, you are perfectly aware that it may not help in the long run to loan anyone money, especially if it only perpetuates rotten financial habits. Ready responses for someone who wants your money include:

- *(With a frown)* "Dash it all. I just put every penny I have into a forty-two-year CD."
- *(With a smile)* "Shakespeare said, 'Neither a borrower nor a lender be.' "
- *(With set jaw and nervous tic)* "Banks earn every penny they make."
- "Sure, I'll loan you money. When pigs say 'moo.' "

In order to help someone establish or reestablish credit, you might consider cosigning a loan. However, the bank won't trouble itself too much chasing down your friend or relative should there be a problem. You will be liable for the loan—and can have your credit record scarred if anything goes very wrong. Watch the small print.

On the flip side, if you have ever taken out a loan from a friend or relative without paying it back, keep in mind that you have no excuse not to pay it back. Tsk! Tsk! Not a word out of you; you have no excuse. But it is never too late to make good.

THEY THINK THEY'RE SO SMART

Local and national credit bureaus periodically ask for information about individuals, and they receive it in due course from credit card issuers, banks, and even bankruptcy courts. A credit bureau serves a purpose, sort of, offering other creditors raw facts about how long you have maintained each of your accounts, whether you have ever been late in making a payment, and what credit limit you have been allowed. The report will also tell your age, what you do for a living, how long you have lived at your current address, and whether you own your home. Bureaus are now using techniques, chillingly enough, to identify and hamper people who are currently solvent but fit a profile of future credit problems.

It's galling to think that a company would stoop to creating a one-page summation of a human spirit, without even taking the time to interview neighbors and old schoolteachers to find the essential wonderfulness of the person behind the printout. If there were even one line in the file for wonderfulness, people might not, in all honesty, despise credit bureaus: "It says here that I'm a code 36, a bankruptcy waiting to happen. But look—they note here that I took that stray puppy to the vet and paid to have it cured. Aww."

Wrongly accused! Sometimes, the raw data at the credit bureau contains a mistake or a fact arising from a total misunderstanding. Let's say you apply for a credit card at your favorite restaurant, Greasy Guy's Tub o' Fries. (You have no secrets in the credit bureau section.) Three weeks later, you get a letter from the Tub o' Fries saying that it cannot proceed with your application, as your qualifications do not meet their standards. It feels like a spatter in the face from the big fryer. By law, however, you can call Greasy Guy and find out which credit bureau gave him the information on which he based his decision. And by law, you are entitled to free copies of your record from that bureau. It may take many another phone call and letter to straighten out any problem in your record, but you can then demand that Greasy Guy reconsider your application. A credit card from the Tub. Now you're in fat city!

WHERE'S THE MISSUS?

Wives, in particular, sometimes suffer where credit bureaus are concerned. Joint-account creditworthiness must extend to both parties, and in many states, a husband's record must reflect on his widow or ex-wife. However, married women should periodically request to see copies of both their own and their husband's credit bureau reports. If they are not both complete and full, it may take a few months to correct the omissions. Do it when time is not of the essence—before an emergency or undeserved embarrassment. By law, creditors cannot discriminate against women, or ask questions that might give them a surreptitious way to do so. No one can ask you, as a credit applicant, your marital status. No one can ask you whether you have children—or whether you contemplate having any. No one can ask you if you receive alimony or child support (though you may decide to volunteer that information as an indication of income).

This summary is for all those who are married or living in a serious relationship:

1. Establish a few credit card accounts in your own name; you can still have joint accounts, too, if you are part of a couple.

2. Request copies of your credit bureau report every few years; don't wait until mistakes within it represent a crisis.

3. Take out a secured loan in your own name; if you are in a couple with several cars on credit, be sure to buy or lease one of them in your own name.

WALDORF SALAD: A SCARY STORY

She was quite a saver, our Minnie, and always paid cash for everything. She worked her way through college, and on those rare occasions when she needed money, she borrowed it from her parents, Al and Myra. After college, she worked and saved. And then, at the age of thirty-three, Minnie had enough money to attain her dream. She was going to buy the Waldorf-Astoria Hotel for $200 million. In piles of cash stashed under her bed, she had all but $14,000 of it. Al and Myra gave her all that was under their bed, $13,900. Minnie needed another $100, and so she applied to the bank for a loan.

"I'm terribly sorry," the banker told her after calling around in search of a credit bureau report on her. "But you don't have a credit history. In fact, you don't seem to exist."

A short argument over that point ensued, but the fact is that the credit bureau won out. Minnie did not exist. Even as she sat across the desk from the banker, she faded from sight and was never seen again.

Moral: Build good credit throughout your working life—not three seconds before you need a loan.

SECURING A SECURED LOAN

Loans are rather invisible, yet there is probably more variety and style available among home mortgages than in homes, and the same may be true of cars—even more types of financing than types of autos at the average dealership.

The first step toward obtaining a secured loan is to maintain stable bank accounts. Don't bounce checks. Demonstrate the ability to save money steadily. If possible, establish an acquaintance with a banker at your branch; ask advice about keeping your accounts in good shape. You will probably benefit from it directly—and indirectly, later on.

The second step is to establish credit accounts through bank card companies, local stores, and oil companies. However, people with too many cards can make a new creditor nervous. What may look like slips of plastic to you, to worldly-wise loan officers may look like other claimants at bankruptcy court. Also refrain from cultivating high credit limits on any cards. It ought to be a sign of your sterling credit, but to old Worldly-wise, it is a tipoff that you plan to go on a mad spree someday.

The third step is to sit down and organize yourself before speaking to any bankers. (Nothing is more excruciating than trying to organize oneself *while* talking to a banker.) Gather all your own records: banking and brokerage statements, pay records, assessments of real property, and any legal documents relating to money owed or owing. The basic questions in each of the following cases (home loan or car loan) will be the same:

1. What money or assets are available for a down payment?

2. What money will be available on a regular basis for monthly payments?

The answers to these two questions will largely determine the amount of money you will borrow.

A Home Loan

Owning a home is an accomplishment. That is probably why many parents end up providing the down payment for their children. They want their kid to have an accomplishment, even if they have to give it to him. Or her. Even so, a home is more than just a financial responsibility. It is a decision about the way you want to live, and it is a complicated process. Requiring the timing and derring-do of a trapeze routine, the financing of a home is a tough act. Everyone in the midst of buying a home walks in a trance and says the same thing: "It might not go through." Everyone who is a friend of anyone who is buying a home then says the same thing, "Of course, it will."

The cost of the home. The **down payment** on a home can be as low as nothing at all (for a Veteran's Administration loan, for example), although 15 to 20 percent is more typical. There are several reasons to try to start with at least 20 percent.

1. Unless you obtain an extremely low-interest loan, you'll save money by paying more up front.
2. In financial terms, the home has a foundation in the

form of the money you already paid into it: the equity. The more equity in a home, the more it can withstand outside economic pressures. A down payment of only 5 percent is a flimsy foundation in case of deflation or the sudden need to sell. A common scenario is that people with low home equity, who have to sell into a falling market, actually have to cough up cash in order to *sell.* The result is sometimes bankruptcy. A heftier down payment can usually match such a squeeze.

Next to consider is the **mortgage.** Some people pay cash for housing, but most take out a mortgage, a loan that uses the home itself as collateral. Savings banks traditionally cater to home buyers, although commercial banks and credit unions are in the fray as well. Some people love a good fray. Others can't abide them; mortgage brokers charge a professional fee for leading prospective home buyers through all the possibilities straight to a likely source of money.

The **monthly payment** will include two parts, principal and interest. *Principal* is the actual amount still owed on the home. The proportion will shift throughout the life of the mortgage, but a $600 payment, for example, may be noted as $475 in principal and $125 in interest. The mortgage is usually paid off in such monthly payments over the course of either fifteen or thirty years. Longer terms of even 100 years are available in some parts of the country. These are tantamount to leases that allow holders to participate in a rising market even without accruing much, if any, equity. The sum of twelve mortgage payments, annual property taxes, and home owner's insurance should equal no more than 28 percent of your total pre-tax income. That's not just a rule of thumb, it's the basis of most mortgages.

Closing costs include the many fees you will pay in order to ensure that nothing goes wrong, that the day you move in is not the day you move out, for legal or structural reasons. Figure that closing costs will end up as 5 percent of the total cost of the home.

NEVER BE NERVOUS

Banker: What is your financial background so that I can make a general assessment of the size of the mortgage we might arrange?

Home buyer: Ha, ha, ha. Eighty thousand in liquid assets, no home equity, since I am renting now. I earn $50,000 before tax.

Banker: Well, as a rule of thumb, you might want to keep $50,000 in liquid assets and use $30,000 for initial costs. As to your monthly payments, we might figure that you would use at the most $14,000 per year, or $1,150 per month, for your mortgage, taxes, and insurance. Depending on the mortgage—if we decide to grant it.

Home buyer: Ha, ha, ha.

Banker: You could look at houses in the range of $80,000 to $100,000. You can either have an adjustable-rate mortgage or a fixed-rate mortgage. If interest rates go down, you might not want to be stuck with a fixed-rate mortgage. We have one other good option, which is a fixed-rate mortgage that can be adjusted one time only to a better prevailing rate.

Also, we have either fifteen- or thirty-year mortgages. If you take the fifteen, you'll have a higher monthly rate, but you'll pay the principal off sooner. Unless you have some hot investment that can make better use of your cash, it's a good idea to take a shorter mortgage. Another way to bring down your overall cost substantially is to opt for biweekly payments instead of monthly ones. That can make a big difference.

One other thing that you ought to know about is that we will want quite a number of points. *Points* are up-front payments, each of which is equivalent to one percentage point of the principal at the outset of the mortgage. When we have too much money on hand and we want to get people to take out loans, we only charge one point. But we'll charge you three or four. You know why?

Home buyer: Ha, ha, ha?

Banker: Because we currently have more people who need loans than we have mortgage money.

Home buyer (getting into friend's car outside): It'll never go through. I was too tough about everything. It'll never go through.

On the other hand. "Putting down roots," which strongly implies home ownership, is more than just an expression in this country. It's a veritable commandment. It's a career move. It's eminently respectable. But it isn't always smart. Renting a house or an apartment is a better deal in many cases. Narrowing your eyes over the ledgers, and forgetting sentiment, consider that money put into a home divides into practical return and investment return. Sometimes, a mortgage payment and the rent payment on a similar home are equivalent and people rush in where angels fear to tread, since "it costs almost the same, anyway." But the money needed for a home doesn't end with the mortgage payments; it has to include taxes, general insurance, and maintenance. Renters usually have all that included in their lease. And so the practical return—decent housing—on ownership can easily cost more than it would on renting. In fact, adding up all the expenses, it may be possible to rent a much nicer place than to purchase anything at the same overall amount.

As to investment return, renters receive none. It is true. However, some home owners don't receive any either: The housing market may decline; they may be poor at maintenance and let the house itself slide in value; or likewise, they may spend too much money on the house, in ways that do not increase its selling price. Renting could be smarter, even where none of those possibilities quite exist. If a swell cottage could be either purchased at $1,000 per month, all told, or rented at $600, the renter would have $400 per month to stash away. The return on investment from housing is usually healthy, but with the exception of a few real estate markets around the country, it hasn't been close to what can be realized from a portfolio of Wall Street stocks and bonds.

Renting undoubtedly has its own downsides: The landlord accuses you of wrecking the whole place every time you so much as make bacon without a splatter screen. The rent could rise prohibitively, or the lease could end for some other reason. And home ownership always seems a comfort for later years, come what may, when you picture yourself eating crumbs by the light of the moon. At least you'll have the house. Lifting the eyeshade and taking your eyes off the ledgers, you may just want to buy a house whether it is a good long-term investment or not. A house gives and receives a special loyalty. But still, it is perfectly possible to put down roots in a rental—so long as the landlord doesn't find out that you let anyone touch the hardwood floors in the process.

An Automobile Loan

One of the easiest loans to receive is an automobile loan. And that is what makes it so hard. If you walk slowly enough through some car showrooms, you will emerge with a car loan. If you make the grave mistake of sitting down—oh, you have a car loan. The reason that some salespeople make it so easy, too easy, to take out a car loan is that they know it will be fully secured by collateral—the car. Of course, they are not in the business of making faulty loans (some are, actually), but it is one of those spheres in American life in which you must keep reminding yourself that you don't want just any old credit. You want a pretty good car and a very good loan.

A dealership's loans for new cars are normally written through the finance arms of the manufacturing companies. One way to put a car on sale is to lower the loan terms, of course. New-car and car-loan customers negotiate on several fronts at once:

1. the price of the car.
2. the options and equipment added as enhancements.
3. the interest rate, loan term, and down payment.

The down payment is usually 10 percent, though it is better to buy a car that you can afford to anchor with 30 percent. A bank will normally charge a slightly lower rate of interest on a car loan than will a dealership, and certainly the negotiation is bound to be more straightforward, since the bank can't start throwing in floor mats just to get a signature. Some people take a loan from their whole life insurance, albeit paying interest rather than earning it on the same cash. In some loan markets, however, self-credit is a good option for those people who trust themselves (to pay themselves back).

Juggling the myriad factors involved in taking out an automobile loan, many people will ask each potential lender for a written statement of the monthly payment schedule, including all initial costs. It makes for a pertinent comparison, but only if the durations of the loans are the same. Keep in mind that if you can't afford a certain car without stretching payments beyond three years, you probably can't afford the car. Long-term car loans are a losing proposition.

The very lease you can do. You understand the auto loan: hefty down payment and the car is yours, so long as you keep making the payments. *Leasing* has turned auto loans upside down.

Used for decades in contracts for heavy-duty trucks and company cars, leases offered consumers a new means of financing, beginning in the 1980s. Some people resisted the idea, preferring the old-fashioned concept of owner-ship. However, nobody who puts a trifle down really owns a new car until the last payment is made, and in the end, the same may also be true of a lease.

In a lease, the driver makes monthly payments for a term of a few years, and the "up payment" (to coin a phrase; everything is upside down in a lease) is due at the end, if the driver decides to purchase the car outright. The cost is ultimately based on an interest rate, just as the loan is, and those planning to buy a car on a loan should always consider leasing. The reverse can't be true, if you don't have enough cash for the down payment. *The best aspect of closed-end leasing (used almost universally for con-sumer leases):* The driver is not stuck with a car that has depreciated beyond hope of recovery. *The worst aspect of leasing:* There is a charge for mileage beyond the allow-ance, typically 12,000 miles per year. So the odometer may creep up faster than expected, dashing all thoughts of a car trip to the Yukon.

HOW TO INTERVIEW A CAR LEASE DEALER

Us: I want that Whippet two-seater. I have done my homework and know that it costs $20,000. Can you do any better?

Dealer: How's $21,000? [We are not amused. However, haggling ensues over the initial cost, or capitalized cost, which includes the car and all options.]

Us: All right, $18,000 for the Whippet. Now, what is the lease rate on it?

Dealer: The manufacturer is offering twenty-four months at $390.

Us: What are you using as the *residual value*? [The residual value is the projection of what the car will be worth at the end of the lease. A lease is roughly constructed by subtracting the residual value from the capitalized cost; the remainder is the amount to be financed through the lease.]

Dealer: We got a residual value of about 52 percent on this baby.

Us (vehemently): Oh, come now! This is practically an exact replica of the car that won the Indy 500 yesterday. You can't think it's going to depreciate. [Check the sports pages before using that exact line, but do consider that some cars hold their value better than others.]

Dealer: A low residual value leaves you more to be financed, it's true. But if you would consider buying the Whippet, then a lease is the way to go. We think the car will be worth about $10,000 in two years. If you think it will be worth more, you can buy it then for our figure, because it will be in the contract of a closed-end lease. If it isn't worth more at that point, just walk away.

Us: You have a point. Now, what is the *money factor* in this lease? [The money factor is an inverted way of expressing the interest rate.] Anything you say, I will multiply by 2,400 to express the number as an annual percentage rate.

Dealer: I know what the money factor is. Anyway, it's .00379.

Us: Times 2,400, that's 9.09 percent. No deal. I could buy a Whippet outright at about 8 percent. I'm a money-factor kind of a hairpin.

> **Dealer:** Is that your moped over there? Trade that in on the Whippet lease, and we'll give you $2,500 for it.
> **Us:** But it's only worth about $12.
> **Dealer:** Friend, I'll do anything that'll get a high interest rate out of you. And at the end of the day, you got to do anything that would get a low interest rate out of me—buying or leasing. I can hide a real high interest rate in a real low monthly payment, but not with you. You're a money-factor kind of a hairpin.

Car Lease Checklist:

1. Initial costs can expand to almost double what is advertised due to premiums and mandatory optional equipment—which is definitely not the same as optional mandatory equipment, or anything else that is truly optional.

2. Normally, the lessor is responsible for repairs, except as covered by the new-car warranty. Complete maintenance contracts can be added, as they can with any car, new or used.

3. Penalties for terminating the lease early will always be high enough to sting, but they should not be ruinous in case the necessity arises.

SELECTED GLOSSARY

Balloon mortgage: A loan whereby the principal is due in five years or less. It is often used by people who know they will be moving or by those speculating on a fast-rising housing market.

Bankruptcy: A court-administered dispersal of assets to repay debt. A person or family will enter into bankruptcy when no longer able to satisfy loans and other credit obligations. It protects the debtor from untimely evictions or repossessions.

Credit insurance: A policy that requires the insurer to pay the outstanding balance on a loan in the event that the borrower dies. *Mortgage insurance* is a variation of the same idea. In both cases, regular life insurance is a cheaper way to protect survivors from the obligation to repay loans. See also *private mortgage insurance,* below.

Equity conversion: A method of generating cash from a home property, sometimes called a reverse mortgage. In an equity conversion, the home owner sells the house, usually to an institution, on an installment plan but remains in the home. It is often a last resort for aging home owners who require extra income.

Home-equity loan: An open-ended version of the *second mortgage* (see below), by which the borrower can borrow money, repay it, or extend credit on a self-determined schedule.

Mortgage-backed securities: Government-issued property loans. The three publicly traded corporations that market such loans are known colloquially as Fannie Mae (Federal National Mortgage Association), Freddie Mac (Federal Home Loan Mortgage Corporation), and Ginnie Mae (Government National Mortgage Association).

Passbook loan: A loan granted by the bank, using funds already on deposit in a passbook savings account as collateral. Under some circumstances, a customer may need money, but be unwilling to disrupt the account. This is a good way to establish or reestablish credit.

Principal: The amount of money still owed at any point during a loan, before added interest.

Private mortgage insurance: A policy that assumes payments to the mortgage issuer if a customer legally defaults on repayment. The premium is attached to the mortgage payment.

Second mortgage: A second loan on the same property. Once a home owner builds up enough payments to have a serious stake in a property, lenders will make a loan using that equity as collateral. It is a risky loan, since default may mean eviction; however, the interest rate charged is generally lower than that on other types of personal loans.

GET IN TOUCH

Bankcard Holders of America
560 Herndon Pkwy., Suite 120
Herndon, VA 22070
703–481–1110
Offers information on specific cards with attractive rates and features, along with material on credit card rights and problems, including women's credit rights.

Consumer Credit Counseling Service
800–284–1698
Provides minor to major assistance with credit problems.

Credit Bureaus: All will send a copy of your credit report for a small fee.

CBC-Equifax
Jefferson Park Rd.,
Middleburg, OH 44130
216–234–3601; **www.equifax.com**

Experian
P.O. Box 2104
Allen, TX 75013–2104
800–682–7654; **www.experian.com**

TransUnion
P.O. Box 390
Springfield, PA 19064–0390
800–888–4213; **www.transunion.com**

Debtors Anonymous
P.O. Box 400, Grand Central Station
New York, NY 10163–0400
Self-help group for people with spending problems.

Mortgage Bankers Association
1125 15th St., NW
Washington, DC 20005
202–861–6500; **www.mbaa.org**
Offers material of interest to those considering mortgage
financing.

SIX FOR THE WEB

www.nfcc.org (National Foundation for Consumer
Credit). Offers help for anyone sliding downhill because
of credit card debt.

www.homefair.com (Homebuyer's Fair). Gives mortgage formulas and interest-rate information, along with
extensive advice, for anyone moving across the street or
the country.

www.intellichoice.com (IntelliChoice). Lists new car costs to dealers.

www.dca.org (Debt Counselors of America). Practical advice on crisis relief, along with help on maintaining good credit. Information kit available, with many publications, including the choice between buying and leasing a car, for example.

www.qspace.com (QSpace) Very simple, highly secure site offering credit reports at the standard industry rate of $8.

www.creditinfocenter.com (Web Nation) Offers wide-ranging credit news and advice on building credit.

Chapter 3

WALL STREET WAYS

YOU MUST REMEMBER THIS

Wall Street investments allow an investor to participate in the natural growth of the economy. . . . As a part of the asset ring, a portfolio should include various industries and types of investments to accentuate long-term advantages. . . . Whether buying on a broker's recommendation or not, an investor should know as much about a stock as about any other large purchase. Some of the factors to be judged are a company's overall position within its industry sector; its price-earnings ratio; debt-earnings ratio; management outlook; profitability and efficiency; products in development. . . . Mutual funds can help investors to diversify or to gain access to otherwise difficult markets (such as international ones). Most mutual funds have incentives that encourage customers to hold them at least four years. . . . In fact, most Wall Street investments should be considered for their potential over at least that much time; jumping in and out is fruitless over the long term.

Wall Street proper is located in the oldest part of New York City. You can buy a pretzel or a Fortune 500 company in the course of a walk down Wall Street. But the greater world of investing known as "Wall Street" includes exchanges and markets located all over the country, as well as ones located nowhere in particular, such as in computer nets. Wherever it is, whatever it is, Wall Street has the slight whiff of danger. It's a place where too much money is poured over too much emotion, and the result can be anything at all. It has killings and witching hours, poison pills, and breakouts.

You may have toyed with breaking out yourself, a bit, and trying Wall Street. Just think of it: there are people who took $2,000 there and turned it into $100,000. People who took $5,000 and turned it into $20 million. Try to do that with a money market fund in less than 250 years or so. All without interrupting a real career—just noodling around and picking winners. And then holding forth at dinner parties about recent purchases.

Wall Street is a way of life, not merely an investment. Every morning, shareholders snap the paper open with something like glee to read really important news: how their stocks did. Yet, as an investment, a Wall Street portfolio can be constructed to be quite predictable over a long period. Results may vary from one year to another, but over ten years or more, returns from diversified portfolios commonly stay well ahead of the inflation rate. They may do even more than that; they could do less, too. But Wall Street investments are the only ones within your ring of assets to participate directly in the economic growth of the country, or even the world. In other words, a strong and dependable asset ring does not avoid Wall Street investments; it requires them.

WHAT'S A WALL STREET FOR?

In descending order of the noble nature of its many roles:

1. Wall Street makes money available to business and government. A corporation issues shares of ownership, known as *stock,* and brokerages help to sell those shares to the public. The proceeds are working capital for the corporation. If the company is new to the market, the stock is called an *initial public offering* (IPO); if the company is old hat, it's just a public offering. *Bonds,* a type of loan, vary widely in the rates returned, depending on the perception of the company's future ability to either repay the money or *default,* leaving bondholders without some or all of their money.

2. Wall Street creates the secondary market for stock and bonds, a process that started out literally at a curb on the side of Wall Street in the 1700s. As soon as stock becomes a YPO ("Yesterday's Public Offering," to coin a phrase)—it can be sold by the original customer. This buying and selling, over and over and over again, constitutes the major activity of Wall Street, in terms of the number of transactions generated. From a corporation's point of view, the secondary market for its stock and bonds is important, because the going prices will influence the success of its other financial activities, including future offerings, of course.

3. Wall Street offers opportunities for moneymaking that are secondary even to the secondary market. In options trading and short selling (both of which are explained in this chapter), holders do not quite own a piece

of U.S. (or world) business, as they do with a simple share of stock or a bond. What they have instead is primarily a stake in the price activity of the underlying stock. It is an important differentiation. Options, short selling, and other tertiary instruments can be used in highly conservative ways to counterbalance the risk of owning actual shares. However, many people play such Wall Street opportunities purely for the excitement and frenzy. That may be all right, too, for some people. But anytime you decide to put your money into Wall Street, you should ask yourself, "What *precisely* do I own?"

EXCHANGING INFORMATION

Started in 1792, the New York Stock Exchange (NYSE) is the business establishment's establishment. A brokerage has to pay a stiff price for a seat that allows it to make trades on the exchange; a corporation has to meet extensive standards in accounting practices in order for its stock to be traded there. The result is a daily auction in about 1,700 stocks, conducted in the frenzy of the trading floor. If you call your broker, Old Malcolm at Brass & Farthing, with an order to buy 100 shares of General Motors, the order will go from his office to the NYSE in a matter of moments. The Brass & Farthing desk at the exchange will either give your order to its trader on the floor—a person in a smock waving, shouting, and looking permanently annoyed—or pass it through the exchange's own specialist in GM. The *specialist* watches the current trading and also looks at a computer screen listing all the orders to buy and all the ones to sell GM stock at that moment. In the trading on the floor or through the efforts of the specialist, shares are matched at the prevailing price. Old Malcolm can receive the *confirmation* of your order within minutes, sometimes within seconds.

If Wall Street were located in Wyoming, and not in New York, then the NYSE would be an old stone stable on the best corner in town. The whole corral out back, however, would be NASDAQ, with no building at all.

Started in 1971, the National Association of Securities Dealers Automated Quotations (NASDAQ) has used computer networks, not trading floors, to make a market, or match buyers and sellers in stocks not otherwise listed on any exchange. A corporation, after all, isn't born great. Most are born in a shed and get up on shaky legs. Because they receive varying degrees of care, some of them have little ribs showing through their skin. Scrawny little hopefuls weren't allowed in the stables, but NASDAQ gathered them in by the thousand. There was always room in the corral—and that's what NASDAQ has been, a computerized corral. The excitement about NASDAQ is that many of the rickety foals of the past generation, such as Microsoft, grew up on the NASDAQ exchange, which gained it a reputation as the center of great growth, especially in technology. In 1998, NASDAQ absorbed the American Stock Exchange, home to many smaller stocks. There have been charges through the years, however, that due to the absence of any face-to-face trading, the pricing of shares can leave the small investor at a disadvantage. In the past, big lots often were traded for a fraction of a point, or dollar, less than smaller lots. The problems have been corrected (several times, in fact)— but the fact is that the NYSE is becoming more like NASDAQ, not the reverse.

For many years, the trading day was well defined, beginning with a bell at 9:30 A.M. and ending with another at 4:00 P.M. Today, after-hours trading is doing away with the bells. Both major exchanges, the New York and the NASDAQ, are heading toward extended market hours, lasting throughout the evening (Eastern Standard Time). Meanwhile, brokerages online can offer trading round-the-clock through in-house or coordinated computer services. The after-hours market will take some time to develop, and you should note that trades may not fetch predictable prices until volume builds. Aside from that, there is another reason to hope that round-the-clock trading will arrive slowly (even though it won't). There used to be a palpable feeling of relief on Fridays at 4:00, when the markets closed and everybody's nerves relaxed. Now there is no escape, and to active traders, it will be just that dramatic: life without nights and without weekends.

If that is supposed to be progress, then why does it look so much like old Sisyphus pushing the rock up a hill?

WHO OWNS EXXON?

If you are one of those people who does not vote for president because one vote doesn't carry an election (as though you *would* vote, of course, if you had the only vote), the following will rub you the wrong way: The fact is that stockholders own Exxon and every corporation under discussion in this chapter. It is easy to allow yourself to think that the upper management owns the company and that you, as a shareholder, are only along for the ride. Quite the opposite. Business history offers many examples of vigorous, well-informed stockholders who demand—and get—excellence in management. Most people only know general headlines about the companies they hold, but you should know your company—*your* company—in as much depth as possible.

BREAKING IN A BROKER

Next time you're in New York, don't bring your stock certificates and expect to sell them at the New York Stock Exchange. In the first place, you'd be trampled underfoot; it's quite crowded and busy. In the second place, people aren't allowed in; only brokers are. That is to say, to find a buyer or become a seller through any of the exchanges for stocks, bonds, and certain other instruments, you have to have the services of a stockbroker. However, as implied rudely above, brokers do necessarily have to be human beings.

About twenty-five years ago, the Securities and Exchange Commission (SEC) changed its rules and introduced open price competition among stock brokerages. Before that, commission rates were standard throughout the industry. However, customers had begun to tire of paying for services they didn't need, like updated reports on llama-belly futures in the Urals or bulletins on the length of the rust drippings on rail cars in Wisconsin. Some customers, after all, buy no more than a little AT&T stock every once in a while, whatever the rust situation in Wisconsin. Those customers were naturally attracted to discount brokerages, which offered reduced prices and services, perhaps some advice, but scant proprietary research. Deep-discount brokers carried the choice even further, offering almost no service beyond access to an order taker at the other end of an 800 telephone line. Online computer services are usually extensions of such deep discounting, by which the customer avoids as much of the cost and bother of a brokerage as possible, typing up the order and placing it, without speaking to anyone at all. Some full-service brokerages now offer customers the option of a discounted, online account.

Recently, many corporations have actually started bypassing brokers altogether, buying and selling their own stock. To build a healthy portfolio, though, you will need some sort of brokerage service. Many people new to investing avoid personal brokers in the full-service or discount categories, not only to save a certain percentage on commission rates but also to avoid the intimidation long associated with the stockbroker's profession. The rap against brokers is that they earn their money on commissions from sales; the more times they dazzle a customer into buying and selling issues, the more profits—for them, if not for you. No decent broker would pressure a customer into making a transaction. Yet there are rootin'-tootin' cowboys out there, and the trouble with dismissing them entirely is that some customers want to be dazzled, and to feel as though they are in the heat of the action. The more typical stockbroker will supply basic guidance and technical expertise, and white-hot tips only as requested.

Looking for a Personal Broker:

1. Ask for recommendations from lawyers, bankers, or accountants whom you trust. Call several reputable brokerage houses and ask to speak to the manager. Explain the type of investing that you intend to do and any special needs you have.

2. Ask for a complete fee schedule. Make sure that the brokerage is a member of the exchanges you intend to use, and that it is a financially sound institution. Some brokerages now offer fee-only accounts, which do not incur commissions on each transaction; the charge is about 3 percent annually on average total assets. They are harder than you'd think to work up into a bargain, financially, but may give you peace of mind.

3. Call or visit each broker personally and describe the business you will probably want to do. Make sure that the broker listens to you. And make sure you comprehend every last syllable of what the broker says.

4. A stockbroker is not a financial planner, though some, especially under fee-only accounts, lean in that direction. (See Chapter 8 for a description of financial planning and planners.)

Online Trading

By trading online, an investor is accepting much of the job of the full-service broker—that is, taking on the obligation to sift through mountains of research in order to find and monitor worthy investments. The commissions are indeed lower, but that can be a dangerous reason for selecting a brokerage. The fact is that online brokerages have become popular, in many cases, with exactly the wrong people: those with scant investing experience or expertise. While the independence of online investing has surged during a prolonged bull market, small, ill-prepared clients may find themselves utterly foundering when the first bad market storm hits. In the first place, they may not have defended themselves against such a possibility, and in the second place, they will have nowhere to turn for advice about how exactly to react effectively to a steep downturn.

For those who will take a serious view of investing, applying brainwork, not guesswork, to their decisions, here are some points to consider in choosing an online broker:

Looking for an Online Service:

1. Thoroughly investigate the company and its own financial standing; understand both its confirmation and arbitration processes.

2. Online services are not as yet full service; most can handle common stock trades on the major exchanges, but not all can broker mutual funds or bonds.

3. Costs are largely based on a flat fee of about $10 to $30 per transaction.

4. Account minimums vary from zero up to $100,000.

5. Most online services have live brokers available to take orders at a further charge, but customers often complain that it takes too long—even hours—to get through on the telephone.

THE BAD BROKER

When we left Martha Vineyard, in Chapter 1, she had just been fired by her sister, Nan, for laughing on company time. "I'll file suit for wrongful dismissal," Martha said over her shoulder as she left the-little-factory-that-doesn't-make-anything.

"You do and I'll tell Mom and Dad," Nan retorted.

With no further legal recourse, Martha went home to the little house she shared with her sister. The next thing she knew, she was in the big chair watching a Finnish baseball game on television.

"Nah, if that was a strike, I'm a reindeer hoof," she growled as she lumbered out of the chair to answer the telephone. "Hello?"

"May I speak to Martha Vineyard?" said the man on the line. "One of your friends suggested I call you, Martha. My name is Ron and I am a certified broker. I don't want to take up your time today, but I would like to know if, in the future, you would like me to keep you informed of some opportunities that come up involving investments paying high rates of return for people who have the funds available."

"High rates of return?"

"Can I ask if you would have funds available? I don't want to waste your time, telling you about the high rates we can expect, if it would be hard for you to free up your cash and take advantage . . ."

"I have over $10,000. Would that be enough?"

"In all honesty, we don't sell stock in lots that small, but I have a . . . where is it . . . something just came in before I called you. I actually called you about opportunities down the road, but if you want to act right now, I can put an order in for you, for $10,000 on the shares we just got in. Would you like that? Then, we could close it out for you at month end, for $25,000, and by then, maybe a really good opportunity will have come up."

Martha was thinking of the look on Nan's face when she realized that her unemployed sister had made $15,000 in less than a month.

"I'll take it—100,000 shares at 10 cents each," she blurted out. Suddenly, there was a horrific, shrieking scream. Nan had come home and was standing by the telephone.

"Has it come to this, Martha?" she sobbed. "Forgive me, I
didn't know you were desperate. You can have your job back."

All at once, Martha realized how close she had come to losing
her money to the sort of con artist who thrives on the outer edges
of stock market investing. She hung up the phone. "You saved me
from a close call," she said to Nan.

"I never thought I would find you like this, all alone and watching Finnish baseball on television," Nan said with a shudder.

The do's and don'ts of naive investing are all don'ts. Don't
ever buy stocks from strangers who telephone (or knock
on the door). Don't commit money to any type of investment sold by strangers. Don't ever give any sort of financial information, such as assets or account numbers, to
strangers over the telephone. Needless to say, you are
feeling stalwart now, when you're relaxed here reading a
book, but such con brokers may well prey on you at a
time when something else in your life has gone awry,
holding out the chance of a quick fix to another problem.
Whenever you are off your guard—watching Finnish
baseball on television, so to speak—be doubly careful.

Broker Glossary. When you place an order to buy or sell,
you can specify that it go to the exchange first thing in the
morning *(market open order)*. Throughout the day, you can
place an order to buy or sell at the going price, whenever
it is received on the exchange *(market order)*. Both market
open orders and market orders ensure you will complete
a transaction (except under extremely rare circumstances). You can also be more choosy, however, specify-
ing the prices at which you will buy or sell *(limit orders)*.

Limit orders stay in effect until either the order is executed or you cancel it. A popular type of limit order is the *stop order* for stock you already have in hand. This designates the lowest price you want to take, in the event that the stock suddenly drops. If the fall is especially steep, you still may get something less than the stop order price, but people in parachutes aren't supposed to complain. Orders are normally sold in quantities of at least 100 shares; anything less is called an *odd lot,* and incurs an extra transaction charge.

Special Translator's Edition: Broker Glossary. A *breakout* is a rise in price after a stock has remained quiet for a long time. To *consolidate* is to sell anything that seems toppy, or risky; it is a turn toward the conservative. A market or stock that is *overbought* is at too high a price; if it is *oversold,* it is at too low a price. If a company is about to be taken over against its will, it may take a *poison pill,* one type of which dismantles the company and sells off the pieces. A *position* reflects ownership of a certain stock, and belief in it, as in "I took a position today in Wells Fargo, preferred." A market or stock that is *toppy* has risen higher than it seems likely to remain. On certain dates, options contracts come due and investors holding them may buy or sell, regardless of the prevailing trends; such a day is called a *witching hour.*

A word about day trading. Day trading is the thrill-a-minute style of money management in which a person takes a position in a stock or other vehicle for a very short term, usually only a matter of minutes. By buying a large lot, the trader can make or lose a fortune with only a small tick on price. In the early 1900s, so-called bucket shops catered to such people—such get-rich-*very*-quick people—by letting them speculate on share prices, although no one in the shop actually bothered to buy the shares. It was, in effect, a bet. And day trading is not much more than that.

THE WAYS AND MEANS

A broker is going to have one important question after all is said and done: What do you want to do? There are many theories on how to make money buying and selling stock. Some people stare into the peaks and valleys of charts of previous performance, looking for support and breakouts. Some wait intently for reports of earnings each quarter, oblivious to everything but the numeral itself: Will it beat expectations?

Some people—this won't surprise you—are contrarians. They certainly are. But in the market that means they purposely buy stocks that are currently out of favor. Some divine trends among *sectors* (industry groups of stocks). According to variations on the theory, a general movement in prices in one sector leads inevitably to a movement in prices in a different one. Quite a few people even look at astrology, just in case Jupiter, that big lump of mush, should take a sudden interest in Du Pont 4.50 preferred. Whichever theory ultimately convinces you to buy a stock, be sure that it doesn't blind you to other considerations entirely. To be sensible about it, choose each stock as though it were an apple, and turn it all the way around, just in case the other side has half a worm sticking out.

How to Buy

Certain characteristics of each stock are so very basic that they are printed in the paper every day in listings by the thousands. If you know what you are reading, however, the tiny type sketches a different picture for each one.

When it says in the paper . . .

52-WEEK		Co.	Divi-	%	P/E	Sales 100s	High	Low	Close	Net
HIGH	LOW	NAME	DEND	YIELD						CHG.
80	21.5	RDQ	—	—	24	1560	74	71	73	−1.75

the Wall Street wolverine thinks . . .

Somebody either made a fortune or lost it this year. Check the close at right. Hmm, could have bought it at 21.5 this very year. Drats!	Never heard of it.	No dividend; hence, no yield. The company is making money; hence, the P/E ratio at right. One could hope that the money is being put to better use than paying dividends.	Not so hot. Is this thing over-heated already?	Me-dium.	Quite a spread on an otherwise quiet day on Wall Street. Remind me to check for news re: RDQ.	Pull-back? Buying op? Has the worm turned? Look into this.

When it says in the paper . . .

52-WEEK		Co.	Divi-	%	P/E	Sales 100s	High	Low	Close	Net
HIGH	LOW	NAME	DEND	YIELD						CHG.
21	16.25	HJV	1.52	8.1	10	13332	19	18.75	18	−.5

the Wall Street wolverine thinks . . .

What a steady Eddy; not going to make a killing here.	Never heard of it.	That could add up. It could.	The bank is paying about 6%.	Good.	Sells a lot and barely moves: widows and orphans.	Narrow range.	Wonder how much it'd have to dip to pay 10%. Wishful thinking: With that P/E, why should it?

Taking stock of it. The *52-week high and low* column describes the stock's movement over the past year. The *company name* is abbreviated, confusingly where possible, such that it is ever a challenge to try to find any company. with A, Am, Amer, Americ, or even American in its title. The *dividend* printed in the paper is the projection for the year, based on the most recent quarterly or semiannual dividend. Some stocks haven't missed a dividend since before the Civil War; others are more . . . let's say, rebellious about it. The *yield* calculates the stock's worth as an income investment, reflecting the annual percentage rate returned by the current dividend on stock purchased at the day's closing price.

The *price-to-earnings ratio,* or P/E, divides the company's overall earnings per share into the price of its stock. It is a basic barometer matching the profitability of the company and the attitude of the market toward it. Montgomery Burlap Mills, Inc., or MBM, has fifty shares outstanding. Making and selling its swanky line of burlap formal wear, MBM earned $200 for the year just ended. Its earnings per share are $4. Get your cotton-pickin' hands (literally, in the case of MBM) off that $4; it's not a dividend. For the moment, it's staying right where it is, safe in the boardroom. The board will decide later whether to declare a dividend with the earnings or to pour it back into expansion. Back to the P/E, the current stock price of MyBurp (as the newspaper listings graciously abbreviate it) is $80. Therefore, the price-to-earnings ratio for MBM is 20.

By its very nature as a ratio, several factors influence a P/E, but the lower it is, the better. A low figure of, say, 2 to 7 is an indication that the stock is underpriced in relation to its ability to generate profits. There might well be other reasons that the stock is underpriced, however. A high figure, of about 15 and above, indicates that the stock price is inflated, purely in terms of current earnings power. The promise of even better earnings in the future is the obvious reason for a bloated P/E, which should not, alone, dissuade anyone from buying the stock.

Completing the newspaper listing, the *sales* figure, the number of shares traded, is listed with either two or three zeros lopped off the end, depending on the particular column description. This figure is important largely as a day-to-day comparison of activity in a certain stock. The *closing price* in the newspaper is usually a composite that includes results from regional markets affiliated with the ones on the major exchanges. The stock can shift dramatically with the next session's opening, so don't get your heart absolutely set on buying anything at the closing price.

SWATTING AT STOCKS

You may develop ideas for stock purchases by snooping around the newspaper listings, reading papers and other publications, talking to your broker, or by noticing at the opera opening that all the best people are decked out in burlap. By itself, each reason is not enough to run out and buy stock. Here are some questions to consider first:

1. **Study the sector.** Who are the competitors, and what is good about *them?* What makes Montgomery Burlap Mills even better? What is the outlook for the whole industry group? How does the current trend of the general economy impact it?

2. **Past performance.** How has Monty Mills grown in the past five years? Have its total sales, earnings, and the stock price grown apace with one another, and what are the implications if they haven't? How did the stock price react to reports of previous earnings?

3. **Current data.** What are the numbers behind the P/E ratio? Is there any chance the price is inflated by high hopes, such that it is going to plummet at the first whisper of weaker earnings ahead? Does the company have more assets than liabilities, overall? Heavy debt can depress the price of the stock, suck off earnings to service the debt, and generally make a company with a low P/E turn out to be a very hollow apple.

4. **Future news.** What kind of people are running the company now, and has a line of succession been established? Does the stock get a lot of attention in the market? (Some stocks are in the spotlight and move more than others with a similar profile.) Based on nearly all of the foregoing, what are the best predictions for a growth in earnings in the coming years, and how much of it does the stock price already reflect?

OZZIE, THE LAST SHIRAZZI

Ozzie Shirazzi was old money, one of *the* Shirazzis. Have you never heard of them? Not surprising. The Shirazzis were so rich that the family name has never appeared in the paper, not since 1510 when the first Shirazzi fell off a galleon, dragged himself onshore somewhere between Florida and Maine, and spoke the immortal words (which do not appear anywhere on the family crest): "It's all mine—you hear?"

For 480 years, it was more than fun to be a Shirazzi. Then along came Ozzie Shirazzi, the boy wonder who recently decided to sell the family holdings state by state (he got a lot for Missouri, at least) and industry by industry, investing all the Shirazzi money in one company. An excellent company it was, too: ComTelePuterPhone Inc., except that it went out of business, taking all the Shirazzi money. Just like that. And what of Ozzie, the last Shirazzi? He is now spending his days wandering around racetracks, looking on the ground for winning tickets that people may have thrown away by mistake. "Hey, bub, you got a tip?" someone asked him recently out at Santa Anita. Ozzie paused and answered loudly, his voice quivering,

Diversify! It doesn't matter how you get your money. They'll never get it off you, if you diversify.

EVERY WEEKDAY, 9:30 TO 4:00

Common stocks are not the huddled masses that their name implies. They are issues tied most directly to the fortunes of the company in question. One share, one vote, for one thing. And if the company does well and feels magnanimous, the common stock can earn a dividend. It doesn't have to, however. Those are two of the characteristics of common stock, but not its most attractive feature where most investors are concerned. Since common stock represents nothing more nor less than a fair share of the company, its price will move easily with the well-being, and the perceived well-being, of the company.

The company can also raise money through the sale of *preferred stock*, which tends to be a sober obligation since it is first in line for a dividend, one that is usually higher than any returned by the common stock of the same company. Preferred stock doesn't move as much in price because its dividend return is not tied to the fortunes of the company; it is fixed quite definitely upon issue, almost like that of a bond. *Convertible stock* is preferred stock that can be traded for common stock, and is thus tied indirectly to the well-being of the company.

When a company decides to *go public*, it is selling stock in itself for the first time. Sales of stock in such companies are called initial public offerings (IPOs), which have an undeserved reputation for being corners of hot action. Most IPOs are nothing but business as usual.

Stocks that pay a dividend often do so quarterly (or sometimes annually or semiannually). About a month before the checks are to go out, the company makes a *declaration* of the dividend amount due to *shareholders of record* on a certain upcoming date. Stocks are said to be *ex-dividend* on that date. You can buy a stock on May 1, sell it on May 3, and still get a quarterly dividend check on June 1, if the stock was ex-dividend by May 2.

Blue chip stocks are those considered to be stable, strong, and relatively unshakable, as far as market tremors are concerned. Any stock can be toppled, and don't forget it.

But blue chips represent the best companies in some of the most basic industries. Some traditionally true-blue blue chips are, for example, Du Pont, GE, Hewlett-Packard, and AT&T. *Cyclical* companies are in industries in which growth is inconsistent, and they are used to making progress in cycles. Oil is a quintessential cyclical, as you can see at the gas pump, where supply and demand changes prices before your very eyes. *Utilities* typically yield a high dividend, and stay well ahead of the inflation rate. *Defensive* stocks fill in the blanks of the homespun advice that runs, "Buy stock in _____. No matter what, people are always going to need _____. It's true, during the bleakest depression, people do need _____. However, they need precisely the same amount of it in boom times, so you won't score any touchdowns with stock in _____." And that's why they call it defensive.

International stocks reflect companies that make most of their earnings in overseas trade and are, depending on the exact nature of that trade, variously influenced by the varying strength of the dollar. To the same end—playing the dollar at the same time as you play a stock—issues in foreign companies can be purchased outright on U.S. exchanges or on overseas exchanges (be aware of special tax considerations), or through different types of mutual funds.

Penny stocks are shares in small or new corporations, often unlisted on any exchange and selling for only a few bucks a share. Penny stocks are not the bunny slopes of stock investing, however. It is hard to find responsible reporting on them, and they do not have to meet strict financial criteria, as do stocks on the major exchanges.

Trading can be quite light, and so disposing of them is sometimes time consuming. Often, the market in a particular stock is made by a brokerage that specializes in that issue. The universal caveat to investigate the reputation of any firm with which you do business (and to which you entrust hard-earned money) goes double and even triple for penny-stock brokerages, which have a knack for folding up and disappearing without a trace.

Growth companies are generally new ones, those foals getting up on their legs. They don't normally pay any dividend and they are risky, needless to say, but have a place in a well-balanced portfolio.

The Divers-o-Plotter. To begin with, it's pretty hard to have a diversified portfolio consisting of one stock. Go into the market when you have the funds available to buy three or four (allowing for a few months, perhaps, to buy each advantageously). A full portfolio can contain as many stocks as you think you can follow, but a dozen is usually more than enough to accomplish a goal. Keep in mind the Divers-o-Plotter below as you build a portfolio. Customize the top row to reflect contemporary conditions and your perception of them, but make sure that check marks are spread evenly around the plotter. (The names in italics are not necessarily recommended, but are merely examples of the type that can be bought.)

INDUSTRY GROUPS

	Oil, Natural Resources	Banking, Insurance	Retailers, Autos	Computers, Telephone	Drugs, Health	Industry Mfg.
BLUE CHIP		Amex		Hewlett-Packard		
DEFENSIVE						Kelloggs
GROWTH				EMC	Amgen	
CYCLICAL			Chrysler			
INTL.	British Petroleum					

Divers-o-Tip: As you invest and build a portfolio, keep a notebook or diary explaining why you have made each transaction. What influenced you? What were you thinking would happen? It will help you to appraise your own thinking and develop a strategy.

FUNDS-AMENTAL INVESTING

As a point of statistical inquiry, how many mutual funds would it take to cover every possible combination of available stocks, bonds, and securities? Whatever the exact number, the world of mutual funds is zooming toward it. Only a few combinations are still left, should you want to join the throng and start a fund. Let's look through the file. The Stocks-That-Don't-Have-an-"e"-in-Their-Name Fund is unfulfilled. The socially conscious Companies-That-Don't-Advertise-Behind-Home-Plate Fund has yet to be organized, despite the imperative.

And the High-Income, High-Growth, Low-Risk, Low-Cost Conservative and Yet Aggressive Fund has yet to be—or has it? According to mutual fund advertising on television and through other media, there are quite a few out there. That fact points up one of the true dangers of investing in mutual funds: Mutual funds advertise themselves in the popular press. Stocks cannot, of course. Bonds cannot. But every fact on Wall Street is true or has been at least once, as reflected by many a mutual fund ad campaign. To quote the nineteenth-century politician Benjamin Disraeli: "There are three kinds of lies: lies, damned lies, and statistics."

Look much further than the advertising of mutual funds. Don't be persuaded by "rated *blah-blah-blah* by *la-la-la*," or "up *xx* percent in *xx* years." There is not time herein to tell you how that, or how three-card monte, really works, but suffice it to say that Benjamin Disraeli is on permanent retainer, if you ever want to buzz him.

Mutual funds started in the 1920s, and the formula hasn't really changed. An investment company buys a portfolio of issues on behalf of shareholders who enjoy the benefits and risks of those issues, proportionally.

In the early days, all mutual funds were intended as highly conservative means for a small investor to spread risk thinly over a market: People could buy a whole bowl of soup, so to speak, even if they couldn't afford more than one ingredient otherwise. As the number of issues available on the various markets expanded, it became impractical for many investors, either large or small, to properly chart opportunities. Mutual fund managers became highly specialized in various markets or sectors. Today more than ever, people buy mutual funds just for the expertise of the fund managers. They can buy their bowl of soup from a highly touted chef.

The first step in choosing a mutual fund lies in defining the objective — both your objective in acquiring it and the manager's objective in operating it. There are about two dozen classifications for mutual funds. The following are some of the important ones:

Growth funds look to appreciate over time through investment in strong, expanding companies. They don't return regular income because the types of companies they hold don't often bother paying a dividend. Investors receive a return upon selling the fund, dependent on the change in the price of the underlying stocks. *Aggressive growth funds* take the foregoing even further, looking for soon-to-be strong companies; that is, they take on more risk in looking for more return. They are usually heavily laden with technology stocks.

On the calmer end of the basic growth fund range are *growth and income funds,* which try to find expanding companies that also pay a dividend. Taking that a step in the same direction, *balanced funds* try even harder to pay a handsome dividend and are managed conservatively in order to reduce risk of loss. *Index funds* are presumably quite easy to manage: The fund owns everything in, say, the Dow Jones Industrial Average (DJIA) or the heftier Standard & Poor's 500. *Bond funds* sometimes concentrate on different municipal and Treasury bonds that offer tax-free income. Sometimes they hold good, conservative corporate bonds for steady income. *High-yield bond funds* hold what they hope are good, but know are risky, bonds paying out more money. *International funds* allow the smallest investor to take part in any number of markets around the world; most are titled by nation or region.

How to Buy

There are two ways to choose a mutual fund, and each way tends to lead to a different set of funds.

Independent method: After deciding what type of fund you want, as outlined only generally above, you can consult a compendium, such as *Morningstar Mutual Funds, Value Line Mutual Fund Survey,* or *Standard & Poor's/Lipper Mutual Fund Profiles.* Each is offered on a subscription basis, with advisories being sent through the mail or via the internet. Most libraries maintain bound volumes while websites operated by each service also catalogue past reports. Each provides information and rankings of most available funds. Major newspapers and the financial magazines print mutual fund rankings, too, frequently in special editions every quarter. Always look at the sports pages at the same time, though. Note that last year's losers sometimes end up as this year's champs, and vice versa. Mutual funds are not sports teams, but the same thing can happen to them. Use rankings of any mutual funds (and other issues, to boot) as a general guide, a reflection of the past, definitely not a promise of the future. Certain types of funds are so cyclical that good results over the recent past are only a bad sign that the buying opportunity is over for the time being.

After you have picked a handful of candidate funds, call up each one to request a prospectus. Mutual fund prospectuses have to spell out priorities in plain English, along with a chart disclosing undiluted facts about the fund.

Many people who go through the effort of choosing a

mutual fund by themselves are naturally drawn to no-load funds. *No-load* funds do not charge a sales commission on shares purchased. Some do, however, impose a load, or commission, on shares sold within a short span of years (that is to discourage people from jumping in and out). By and large, no-loads are sold directly by the investment company, whereas load funds are sold through brokers. The load varies, but is likely to be between 5 and 8½ percent—no higher, according to the law.

Dependent method: Having established certain general or quite specific ideas of your own, you can speak with a broker, who will be familiar with various funds, their objectives, and performance. Even when letting the broker select a few that are appropriate, you should still make it your business to look over the prospectuses and have a say in the final decision. It behooves the broker to recommend load funds, since they return most of the commission to none other than the broker. Yet, even if you are looking for something quite arcane, a decent broker will point out no-load funds that fit the bill.

Pricing: The idea behind any mutual fund is to buy and hold a portfolio on behalf of shareholders. Beyond that, there are two types, generally known as *open-end* and *closed-end*. Shares in an open-end fund are unlimited, inasmuch as the investment company can sell as many as it cares to. No one trades them; shares are purchased from the investment company and are sold back to it. The price per share is an absolute, computed by adding up the value of the issues within the portfolio and dividing it by the number of mutual fund shares outstanding. That is the basic price of each share, the net asset value (NAV), listed in the paper. The outperformer of all outperforming mutual funds does not have an NAV that is inflated simply because the fund is popular. It is solely dependent upon the value of the underlying issues. However, practically all funds charge a management fee of about .5 percent annually on the total assets in the fund, and the outperformer will perhaps hike its fee, as a premium. The open-end fund can be load or no-load, as described above.

A second option in mutual funds is the closed-end fund, in which a set number of shares are issued and then traded on one of the exchanges. The pricing of the closed-end fund is dependent on the value of the underlying issues, but fluctuates with the mood of the market, as well. Many closed-end funds traded on the NYSE are country funds, investing in stocks from India, say, or Ireland.

CORPORATE BONDS

Bonds, like water, are everywhere that the human race is, at least in the United States. That is a biological fact. The federal government issues bonds. Local governments issue bonds. Companies issue them. Utilities subsist on them. Individuals have been known to emit them, too. All bonds are instruments of lending; most are negotiable, that is to say, they can be easily sold. The entity that issued it will normally pay the interest throughout the full term but return the principal only at the end, when the bond matures. At that point, with most bonds, the actual piece of paper has to be surrendered.

Bonds are sold on the secondary market, just as stocks

are. As a first step, investors note the interest rate at which the bond was issued, take a look at the rates on new issues, and then decide how much they want to spend for the old bond. U.S. Treasury bonds trade on the secondary market, fluctuating almost purely on the basis of prevailing interest rates. They are excellent savings vehicles, being eminently safe (as discussed in Chapter 1).

Corporate bonds and municipal bonds are traded with an extra dimension: How good is the company behind the bond? If Tim buys a bond issued by Andy and then tries to sell it to Sarah, she may bypass the first question always related to Treasury bonds (what rate of interest is it paying?) to cut to the point: Who's Andy and how likely is he to skip out on payments? Corporate and municipal bonds are rated by specialist firms that try to answer, in just three letters, the basic question, "Who is Andy?" Firms such as Moody's and Standard & Poor's analyze the entity behind each of thousands of bonds popularly traded. The result is the rating, the all-important rating. The firms use slightly different criteria, but typically have at least a dozen gradations, Aaa or AAA being the highest at the firms mentioned, and something like Baa, in the slush, lower down. Poorly rated bonds have to pay a higher rate of interest on issue; those most disdained are called high-yield bonds or junk bonds. Junk bonds aren't necessarily bad, though. If mortgages were ranked like bonds are, then there would be many people listed as "junk home owners," yet they are good people who will satisfy the debt. Junk bonds have to be investigated carefully, but they can be good, too.

A change in rating over the life of the bond will drive the price up or down. Bond prices are not directly affected by most daily bits of company news, and so they are not quite as glamorous as common stock.

OPTIONS

The option is an opportunity to buy or to sell stock shares by a certain date for a certain price. Take a chance, right now, and spend $3 for an option (expiring September 1) to buy a share of Broadway & Off-Broadway Organization, Inc., stock for $100. You can *exercise* (trade-in) that option with $100 at any time up to September 1 for a share of BOFFO. If BOFFO is selling for only $90, there would be no use in that, though, would there? If, however, BOFFO opens a lost Cole Porter musical on August 10 and its stock suddenly shoots up to $150, you can sell your option, just your $3 option, for something like $50. The option to buy is known as a *call*.

An option to sell is exactly the opposite and causes the bearer to root for the stock to go down. For example, it would be bliss to own an option to sell BOFFO at $100, if the musical turned out to be by Cole *Q*. Porter (no relation) and BOFFO sank to $50. The option to sell is called a *put*. There's one last vitally important thing to consider. If BOFFO goes the wrong way (if it goes to $200 and you have an option to sell it at a paltry $100) and then the expiration date comes and goes, what you have then looks in the mind's eye like a match that just went out. And is worth precisely the same amount of money.

If you think about it, however, you can see the conservatism in the option strategy by which you buy BOFFO common stock outright, along with a put to cover yourself in case the stock price goes down.

Selling short is another way to root for a stock to go down in price. How to short BOFFO? Borrow a share from the brokerage when it is selling for $100, sell it immediately, and pocket the money. Wait until word gets out that Cole Q. can't rhyme, and then buy a replacement share at $50 to return to the broker. Imagine the sweet loneliness of having sold short right before the stock market crash of 1929. Stocks do go up, though, in which case, short sellers go down. For the count.

The brokerage can either lend shares for short selling or money for stock buying. That loan is called a *margin,* by which the customer pays at least 50 percent of the cost of the stock and is charged interest on the difference.

HOW TO LISTEN TO THE FINANCIAL REPORT

Oddly enough, it's the things that are said every day on television and radio that are hardest to understand. Most people can be present for the whole weather report, without absorbing any two consecutive words until the forecast at the end. By that time, talk of pressure systems has already put the aforementioned people to daydreaming. Financial reports are becoming just as common on the news, but to what effect? Most people understand the big arrow. It's usually yellow, if it is going up. Sometimes it's red, if it is going down. And then they say things. But nobody need tune out. Here are three of the usual catchphrases brought to you in living color:

The *Dow Jones Industrial Average* (DJIA) reflects the

prevailing mood of the market. The Dow, as it is commonly known, is based on the prices of thirty stocks, weighted carefully to provide a microcosm of very big Big Business in this country. Before you daydream, ponder this: Did the Dow go up or down by a couple hundred points? Since the crash of 1987, trading curbs have been in effect, such that when the Dow moves dramatically in either direction by a couple hundred points, computerized trading is limited for the rest of the trading day. The only stock still included on the Dow since its inception in 1884 is GE. Neither it nor the complement of stocks on the Dow Jones Industrial Average is completely industrial anymore, however. You can buy a mutual fund that exactly mirrors the composition of the Dow.

The *Dow Jones Transportation Average* reflects twenty stocks that describe another side of the economy. When you compare the movement of the Dow (Jones Industrial Average) with the (Dow Jones) Transportation Average and see that they are going the same way in the same measure, it could spell a *trend*. A trend! A trend! A trend is the weather front of Wall Street. It could be coming this way or suddenly move north just before it gets to your place.

The *thirty-year Treasury bond rate* is expressed in two ways. But first, an interruption to answer the most important question of any paragraph, especially this one: Who cares what it is? Should you bring an umbrella to lunch, depending on what the thirty-year rate is? No. Will it change the price of lettuce? You needn't rush out to the market. And yet, the thirty-year Treasury is a jolly great thermometer, taking the temperature of the U.S. economy. It describes the worth of the safest of investments, and so, as a figure, it is generally bumped back and forth between the two answers to one basic question: Could I make money more easily and safely elsewhere? If yes, the rate tends to go down or stay the same; if no, it tends to rise. Just consider these points:

1. If the interest rate leaps, wait about three seconds, and you're likely to hear from a Wall Street analyst talking about fears of inflation. Time it with your watch next time.

2. Home mortgages and other variable rate loans are attached to the thirty-year Treasury rate, and so it affects personal spending across the country.

3. A slowly rising interest rate on the thirty-year Treasury can indicate that there is less interest in Wall Street, and a quickly rising one is perceived as a mob rushing for shelter in fear of a coming thunder-boomer. (Or low-pressure system, as they say in the weather reports.)

SELECTED GLOSSARY

Commodity: Any raw material traded as an investment. Major commodities are corn, cotton, sow bellies, frozen orange juice, and so forth. The Chicago Board of Trade is the major commodity market in the United States.

Convertible bond: A bond that can be exchanged for stock by the holder. That type of bond floats with the price of the company's stock more than does a standard bond.

Debenture: A bond backed by the general credit of a company, rather than issued against some collateral. A debenture is unsecured, in that sense. It is normally issued by a company of long and fine standing.

Par value: This represents the original price or value of a stock as printed on the certificate. It does not necessarily reflect the current price.

Prospectus: The legally proscribed sales material for a security or other investment. The prospectus is famously dull reading, but it is a precise outline and a source of important information.

Securities and Exchange Commission (SEC): The monitoring body that oversees individual securities (stocks, bonds, and related instruments) and the markets that cater to them.

Split: The division of all shares outstanding, with a proportional reduction in their price. Typically, a split will give the investor two shares for each one held on a certain date; the price per share will simultaneously drop by half. Many companies like to maintain a stock price in a certain range. If the price rises substantially above that range, the board of directors can declare a split to position the price according to their predilections.

GET IN TOUCH

Bond Investors Association
P.O. Box 4427
6175 NW 153rd St., Suite 229
Miami Lakes, FL 33014
305–557–1832
Lists current rates and trends. Newsletter available by subscription.

Investment Company Institute
1401 H St., NW
Washington, DC 20005
Represents the mutual fund industry, but offers consumer-related material.

North American Securities Administrators Association
1 Massachusetts Ave., NW, Suite 310
Washington, DC 20001
202–737–0900
Trade group for state government regulators of investor fraud. It can answer questions about specific brokerages. Send for list of brochures.

Securities and Exchange Commission
202–272–7450

SIX ON THE WEB:

www.sec.gov (Securities & Exchange Commission). Offers annual and quarterly reports as filed by publicly traded companies. Since the access codes are confusing to many people, a site called **www.FreeEdgar.com** gives users simplified access to the SEC filings.

www.ici.org (Investment Company Institute). Extensive background information on mutual fund investing, along with industry statistics.

www.morningstar.net (Morningstar, Inc.). Along with current market data, the site features in-depth analysis of trends, updated daily, as well as information on thousands of mutual funds.

www.gomez.com (Gomez Advisors). Ranks online brokerages and lists the current services of each. It also reviews and ranks other online financial services, including banks, auctions, insurance and travel services.

www.investinginbonds.com (The Bond Market Association). Education on the full range of bond investment, the topics starting with the simplest questions. Also, **www. moodys.com** (Moody's, Inc.) is a source for current data on thousands of bond issues. Finally, **www. savingsbonds.gov** (U.S. Treasury) will explain all of the options in U.S. savings bonds, and calculate the worth of any that you already hold.

www.siliconinvestor.com (Silicon Investor). One of many sites featuring up-to-the-minute investment information. Other popular ones are the more hectic **www.wallstreetcity.com** and the more detailed **www.clearstation.com.**

Chapter 4

INSURANCE

Most forms of insurance are "term" policies. They offer coverage as long as payments are up to date but cease to exist otherwise. Car and homeowner insurance policies are examples. Life insurance can be written as a term policy. However, it can also be written to incorporate a savings plan in a whole life policy. . . . Men and women who have other people dependent on their incomes should absolutely have life insurance coverage. People without dependents normally do not need life insurance. . . . Health coverage is often part of work-related benefits. Two types of coverage sometimes overlooked are disability and long-term care coverage. . . . Insurance is just as important for renters and owners of co-ops and condos as it is for householders. . . . Automobile insurance varies state by state; look especially hard at the bodily injury liability and uninsured motorist provisions of your policy.

INSURE . . . TO BE SURE

Insurance is a highly civilized innovation. It must be, because it can't be natural to write checks to big companies in the hope that you won't get anything in return.

Consider life without insurance. Daniel Defoe described a seventeenth-century house fire in *Moll Flanders*. At the first sign of flames, all the neighbors came running . . . and went off running, carrying home all the good stuff. A few people had insurance in those days, but for most, the best way to replace losses was to wait for the next house fire.

The idea of insurance was sensible and clever. How could it not be, since the first successful insurance company in America was started by Ben Franklin? His company, started in 1735 to offer fire insurance for homes, had a fitting slogan: Hand in Hand. (Even then, insurance company advertising was sappy.) Firefighting grew out of such fire insurance companies. They began to develop portable apparatus in about 1800 to protect the homes of policyholders.

Considering that the insurance industry can be notoriously high-handed in dealing with individuals, it has been a sturdy advocate throughout the years for whole classes of people. Much of the most effective social work of the last century was done by insurance companies, which improved health and safety in the home one family at a time. It was in their interest to improve profits, of course, but it was also important because no one else at the time was so pointedly concerned with the welfare of the underclass. And by the beginning of this century, insurance companies had the same marked effect on the safety of the workplace.

An attorney in Buffalo, New York, once observed that people buy insurance for two reasons: either because they need it or because they want it. Usually, he said, they buy the right policies when they concentrate on what they need, but throw their money away when they reach out for what they want. Insurance companies got that news long before it reached Buffalo, and so you should decide very soberly what you need. Don't get anything less, but getting much more is a waste. And Ben Franklin would surely disapprove of wastefulness.

A LITTLE BIT ABOUT LIFE

People probably learned more about life insurance from the suspense movie *Double Indemnity* than from any company brochure ever printed, mostly because the man who was insured barely appeared on screen. The audience was more concerned with his platinum blond wife, and she was more concerned with the insurance agent, and that is the basic plot of the movie. An actual *double indemnity* is a clause that stipulates a payout that is twice as big for an accidental death as it is for, say, death from disease. If your policy includes such a clause, do not stand near the door on moving trains.

And if your wife wears an atrocious platinum blond wig, you may be better off without any life insurance at all. Other than that, however, people who need life insurance cannot ignore it for any reason.

The basic mechanism of life insurance is that the *benefi-*

ciary receives a large sum if the policyholder goes south. Many women shirk life insurance, even though they have dependents. That can obviously be a disaster for survivors already thrown into disarray. Overall, though, it is a clear indication of the worth that such women place on themselves, and that is dismaying.

The rule regarding life insurance is among the simplest. If anyone at all is dependent on your income, you need a good policy. Typical dependents are children, aging relatives, and a spouse. Couples require coverage whether or not both people are employed when both incomes are needed to pay a mortgage or other expenses, for example. Single people with no dependents whatsoever do not need life insurance, unless they don't have the assets (between $5,000 and $10,000) for a decent send-off, or unless they own a business that is dependent on them to retain its worth. A single person who buys life insurance anyway, as some sort of bonus check for surviving relatives, is buying insurance that may be wanted but is not needed.

Weighing Yourself

Climb onto the scale like a prize steer so that you can see what you are worth on the hoof. A life insurance policy can be written to pay out almost any amount, with corresponding premiums. Consider the payout (the death benefit) carefully and don't be distracted by the savings features that are available in some policies. These are the very basic questions:

1. What is your value, monetarily? (Or just how much do Alfie, Markie, Mitsie, and Joan require?) Project what your survivors will need, basing the figure on what you spend on them currently. Include upcoming expenses, such as college tuition, in addition to outstanding debts, such as the remainder owed on a home mortgage, if payments are your responsibility. Business debts must be handled carefully, perhaps with a separate policy, since the inability to pay them could result not only in the failure of the business but also in the personal bankruptcy of surviving family members.

A simplified example: Cora is the sole provider for her husband, Alfie (who has been working on his next play ever since they got home from the honeymoon) and their three children. She spends $80,000 per year to support them all. Social Security and company pension benefits will provide $20,000 per year, leaving a $60,000 nut to be covered annually. Conservative investment of about $1 million would produce that much. In addition, Cora intends to leave $100,000 per child to cover college tuition. Cora wants to leave $1.3 million, enough to pay for absolutely everything—except Alfie's trips to Club Med.

2. What is your worth, monetarily? (Or how much does Cora already have?)

Cora has $200,000 in savings and investments. Subtracting that from the $1.3 million that she needs, she will begin looking for a policy with a benefit of approximately $1.1 million. Note that a million dollars sounds like a lot of money, especially since life insurance payouts are not subject to income tax. Spent all in one day, a million dollars is a fortune. Used as a source of income, though, it is only equal to the earning power of one middle-class worker.

The amount of life insurance that you need changes with your age, family situation, job status, and other assets. It's a dull little thought, but one that has bought many a bad agent a beachhouse on Maui or Hilton Head. Agents make a lot more money selling a new policy than in anything else. Don't let one churn you—pleasant image, eh?—by talking you into a new (whole life type) policy, if all you need is an adjustment to your old one. In board-game terms, "churning" is returning to Go without collecting $200, and in the near past, agents have gone directly to jail for perpetrating it.

JUST TO EASE YOUR CONSCIENCE

The basic, sturdy bicycle of life insurance is the *term policy*. It was invented in the last century to do the obvious. As long as the holder keeps peddling—which is to say, keeps paying a monthly premium—it works; it will pay a lump sum to the beneficiary. However, it is a cash-and-carry business; nothing in the way of savings is stored over the course of a term policy.

Your first step in buying term life insurance is to decide whether you plan to remain in the pink. It's entirely up to you.

If you decide to remain perfectly healthy for the rest of your life, the *level term premium* policy locks in a certain benefit at a certain premium for a preset term ranging from one to twenty years. The fact that the premium will not increase during the course of a term makes the policy quite tantalizing. After the first term, however, the company may want you to pass another physical exam before it will extend the policy, so you'd better stay healthy. Many frugal people, particularly single parents, buy a hefty twenty-year term policy when their children are young, and do not even bother to renew at the end when the children are grown and have no further need of their parent's life insurance. Some parents reading this may be rather amazed to think that children can really be grown-up and self-supporting after only twenty years. In cases where it happens, however, level premium term life serves its purpose neatly.

If you decide that you can't decide whether or not you'll be healthy for the rest of your life, the *annually renewable term* policy will remain in effect as long as the premiums are paid. It can't be canceled on any other basis. The premium for an annually renewable policy is apt to start out low and then rise quite steeply after the policyholder reaches the age of about sixty.

LIVE LONG AND PROSPER

Can it be true, as the surveys report, that most people do not think they are ever going to . . . to . . . go south? Understandably, it is unnatural for human beings to imagine life going on without them; the survival instinct kicks in and denies the possibility. The insurance companies, in their philosophical purity, figured that out a long time ago, and noted that humans are much happier when they are thinking about themselves, and more to the point, thinking about themselves being alive. That is one of the major selling points of whole life insurance. Most of the discussion pertains to how and when the *policyholder* will get the big payout. A tiny, quiet part of the discussion mentions how the survivors may, perhaps, receive that other payout (the death benefit).

The *whole life* policy costs more than the term type, but

it incorporates a savings plan within the premium structure and forms a long-term partnership with the company. The purpose is to provide either money for you to live on in your dotage or a suitable benefit for your survivors, in the event that you don't make it as far as dotage.

Since a whole life plan results in the accumulation of savings, with a life insurance provision incorporated into it, a policy can be basic to financial planning on both fronts. However, term life insurance in concert with careful savings in an IRA-type account will be even more effective in both respects. The main exception to that rule is the very rich person facing particular problems in estate planning. The other exception often mentioned is the person who needs the discipline of a whole life policy in order to save any money at all. People who don't have the discipline to save often don't have the discipline to pay a large premium, either, accounting for the fact that the majority of whole life policies lapse for nonpayment within ten years. That's very sad.

You may well find yourself pressured by an agent into buying a whole life policy, since they are much, much more profitable for companies—and for insurance agents.

What's whole life? (And when was the War of 1812?) Whole life covers the policyholder's whole life. It can't be canceled, in the first place, and in the second, the premium is locked in as part of the initial contract. It starts higher than the premium for annually renewable term coverage carrying the same benefit, but it ends up lower. For a person at age twenty-five, the term policy may be $10 per month, whereas a whole life policy is $150. However, by the time the policyholder is, say, sixty, the same type of term policy premium might be $350 per month, whereas the whole life premium will be . . . still $150.

QUIZLET

Let's take the case of Cora and Alfie (whom we met earlier). Cora is twenty-eight, but she knows she will receive a $1.5 million trust fund at the age of thirty-five. (Bully, bully for her.) That would change the type of policy she needs. When Cora is twenty-eight, and knows that she will no longer need life insurance when she is thirty-five, should she buy a term policy or a whole life policy for the interim?

(Four seconds left . . . three . . . two . . . pens down, please.)

Answer: Term. All other things being equal, it will be cheaper. She need not pay into the savings plan of a whole life policy, because she won't get back any of it after only six years. In fact, a whole life plan should never be considered as a short-term option; the savings aspects of the whole life plan do not begin to gather steam for at least ten or fifteen years.

Bonus Quizlet

Should Cora get level term or annually renewable term life insurance? (If you get this right, you may have a five-minute break, while everybody else rereads Just to Ease Your Conscience.)

Answer: Annually renewable would have a lower premium for a person in Cora's age bracket (28–35) than a level term.

Prying Loose the Money

To reiterate, a term policy pays only under one circumstance: the big one. However, a whole life policy can return money in any number of ways. First the relatively fun ones:

• *A loan from your policy.* You'll pay interest to your good friend and partner, the insurance company, but you can borrow money that has accumulated on the policy without disturbing its obligation to pay a death benefit.

• *Cashing out.* You can take the money that has accrued and terminate the policy. The amount may not be much because the savings portion of your premium is weighted toward the end of the life of the policy.

• *Redeeming the policy.* On reaching an age stipulated in the policy, usually sixty-two or sixty-five, you can surrender the whole life policy and receive either a lump sum or an annuity from that sum.

Now for the not-so-fun ones:

• *Living Benefits.* If a policyholder has a catastrophic health problem, many insurance companies will pay most of the death benefit in advance; the amount is discounted by up to about 25 percent. Basically and bluntly, a person has to be dying to get *living benefits,* with a specific diagnosis for a terminal disease. Circumstances may preclude choice, but one should try not to resort to the use of living benefits to defray medical expenses. It may leave dependents destitute, which is never the desired result in taking out life insurance. Good, extensive health-care coverage should take care of expenses while one is alive, and life insurance should be left for the dependents.

• *Death Benefit.* The survivors need only prove that the policyholder is gone in order to collect a big check. However, the policyholder, who knows the future survivors very, very well, may prefer to stipulate that benefits be disbursed in monthly checks.

Whole Life Tips

Hard times: If you skip a premium payment, the policy remains in effect, except that the company removes the premium amount from the cash that has accrued in your policy. That's comforting to know, just as you trip into the piranha tank. However, read on.

No lapse time: Many people assume that if they stop paying premiums altogether, the money already accrued in the policy will just sit tight until it is cashed. As a matter of fact, the company continues to extract premiums from the policy until it is all gone. If it appears that you are definitely sliding down that route, it is much better to cash what is left of the whole life policy and buy less expensive term life insurance.

MONEY IN THE BANK

A whole life policy is, in part, a giant mutual fund. The base part of the premium goes into the costs associated with insuring the policyholder's life: a cash reserve against payouts and investments on behalf of future payouts. The company invests the rest of the premium in all sorts of securities and businesses, encouraging the policyholder to consider that as long-term savings.

It is time to consider what happens when death strikes . . . the company. There are two ways disaster can strike a life insurance company. First, too many policyholders could possibly die all at once, wiping out the cash reserve and toppling the other investments. That is not likely. Companies know all there is to know about life expectancies across a large group of people. Second, the value of the investments constituting your savings may vary inordinately. If it decreases too much, an insurance company can, and sometimes does, go bankrupt. The long-term survival of a company matters much more for holders of whole life than term life insurance. Insurance companies are rated by such firms as Moody's and Best's. Your lawyer or broker can usually check the ratings for you, or you can probably find them through your library.

In the olden days of conservative money management, policyholders wanted rock-solid protection from their life insurance. They did not want thrills from it. And it can be said with utter certainty that there are few entities so lacking in thrills as either term or basic whole life insurance. More recently, however, two types of policies have become popular, both offering something of the risk and reward of investing.

In a *variable life policy*, the company invests premiums as wisely as it can and passes the resulting profits or losses back to the policy, in both the amount of savings accrued for eventual redemption and in the amount of the death benefit, should it come to pass during the life of the policy. There is a floor below which the death benefit cannot sink, no matter the weakness of the investments; however, the variable life is still riskier than the standard whole life policy. The *universal life* policy is similar to the variable, except that the policyholder directs the investments personally. Both types of accounts charge a management fee in addition to the premium. Both compromise insurance protection in favor of investment growth that you can find elsewhere. Before buying either variable or universal life insurance, weigh the choice against the inherent wisdom of buying term life insurance instead, and putting the difference into a well-managed brokerage account.

WHAT PEOPLE THINK ABOUT WHILE MOWING THE LAWN

Whole Life Policyholder: I get me $100,000 when I hit sixty-five and I'm getting an R.V. with a picture of a fox on the back. No, a hawk. No, a . . .

Variable Life Policyholder: I wonder what in blue tarnation I'll get when I hit sixty-five.

Universal Life Policyholder: I knew I shouldn't have put more money into that pathetic common stock. I should've sold it all and bought T-bonds. Actually, I should've . . .

Term Policyholder: If I had whole life insurance, I'd have something to daydream about. As it is, all I have is insurance.

JASPAR PROVES HE CARES

Jaspar did not earn much money, but he was a good dad to his baby girl, Oona. Except for one thing. He put off buying life insurance. (Don't worry, this story does not have a sad ending.) Then Jaspar's wife, Lettie, gave birth to twins, who were named Two-na and Three-na. Jaspar, the sole wage earner in the family, figured out that he could afford $100 per month for life insurance to protect his four favorite people. For that amount, the insurance agent, Mrs. Dunwiddy, told Jaspar that if he put $100 per month into a whole life insurance policy, he would have $120,000 when he retired. Jaspar was unfazed. He asked what the death benefit would be in that case. "One hundred thousand dollars," Mrs. Dunwiddy said.

"I am not buying insurance for my sake," he said slowly. "I'm here to provide for Lettie, Oona, Two-na, and Three-na. That $100,000 will give them an income of about $6,000 a year if I'm gone. That's peanuts. How much would a term life insurance policy pay for the same premium?"

"Six hundred thousand dollars," was the answer.

"They'll get an income of around $36,000 from that. *That's* why I'm here in the first place."

"But you won't have anything left when you retire, after making payments all through the years. You must consider that, and the fact is, the odds are very good that you will live to be sixty-five."

"I'll worry about me some other time," Jaspar said, "Life insurance is for them."

HOW TO BUY LIFE INSURANCE

Most people would rather die than talk about life insurance. However, that is not a viable option. If you really can't bear to do anything more than the minimum, here's better-than-nothing advice: Call two or three agents at highly rated firms or a couple of independent agents and request a telephone quote for annually renewable term life insurance paying a death benefit equal to eight times your annual salary. That is a rudimentary method of covering your family, but this book seeks to be realistic about the fact that some people have to toddle before they can run.

If you have a fairly complex financial situation, or specific needs regarding your dependents, speak first to a financial planner (see Chapter 7). The same could be said of any of the long-term decisions in this book, but life insurance has facets and tax implications that may require the advice of a disinterested expert—in other words, not necessarily an agent who sees the world through insurance-colored glasses.

In simpler, more standard transactions, a good insurance agent will normally have to know quite a lot about you before suggesting policies and benefit amounts. Dismiss the advice of any who presume to suggest what you need without really knowing who you are. In some states, *savings banks* offer straightforward life insurance. Clubs and professional organizations often offer *group coverage,* in which you will not have much choice. However, since the group actually owns the policy, the rates are usually good and a medical exam is not required.

A HEALTH COVERAGE PRIMER

In the family mentioned earlier in this chapter, Cora was bringing in about $80,000 to take care of her no-talent husband (but a nice guy) and their three children. Unexpectedly, she developed a debilitating medical problem that forced her to quit working at the age of twenty-nine. Her $80,000 per year ceased. And yet, to make a crass observation, she still expected to keep eating. The four others also expected to keep eating. Cora didn't want to move her family, but she had to, and quickly. It was devastating. Alfie yelled and told her not to eat anymore. Fortunately for Cora, it was only a nightmare this time, and when she woke up, she ran out and bought *disability coverage.* First, she had a four-egg omelette.

Disability coverage is as important as life insurance; it replaces about three-quarters of the salary of a person who can't work for a long period of time. The longer the delay for the first payment following the disability, the less such policies cost. If you keep a year's income in fairly liquid form (as suggested in Chapter 1), you can buy reasonable disability insurance that initiates payment after one year. Disability coverage is a bridge between two much more prominent forms of insurance: medical and life.

Edging further into medical insurance, a *long-term care* policy insures people who have to have a nurse at home or who need to live in a hospital setting for months or years. People can live in luxury hotels in Paris for less than some long-term care facilities—and not many families can afford to send one of their own on a five-star sojourn in Paris for a year or longer. Families get wiped out; the government's Medicaid program may step in to pay the bills, but not until the family coffers are nearly empty. If you can keep your emergency fund (of a year's salary) available, you can buy a policy at a relatively low cost, set to take effect three months after the care begins. Everyone in the family should be covered for long-term care, not merely the provider(s).

The U.S. government provides medical coverage to two major groups: to the poor through *Medicaid* and to those over the age of sixty-five through *Medicare*, with caveats applying to both. Children in certain circumstances have recently been brought under the umbrella, as well. Some people who fall into none of these categories neglect to buy health insurance on the presumption that they can always hurl themselves on the mercy of some kindly hospital or on the government should they, say, contract orange disease, getting thick orange skin and rounder by the minute. However, such a patient will almost surely be part of a mimosa by the time the government verifies that he and his family—and everyone who ever signed his high school yearbook—is really and *truly* too poor to support him. And as to kindly hospitals, you will roll far and wide before you find one willing to take in a serious case like orange disease in this day and age.

The traditional source for health coverage has been the standard insurance company, or *indemnity company*. It did not take care of the patient; it took care of the expenses. Indemnification is the obligation to assume such expenses. Health insurance coverage that is advisable includes interlocking, overlapping, and largely baffling parts: hospitalization, surgical procedure, and office visits (the three together being known as *basic*), and Major Medical (all four being known as *comprehensive*). Listing them somewhat differently:

• So your relatives don't have to sell their houses: Major Medical covers the ongoing treatment of almost any malady or injury. Policies usually provide at least $1 million in expenses over the policyholder's lifetime.

• So you don't have to sell your house: Hospitalization pays for a limited stay, including room and board, normally followed by a list the size of a bedsheet noting procedures and supplies, down to the last, individually coded Band-Aid.

• So you don't have to sell your car: The surgical procedure part pays the doctor, whether the service was rendered at the hospital or an office. Doctors and insurance providers have been known to disagree about what was done and what it was worth. Discuss the costs with the insurance provider in advance of the procedure, if possible, to avoid being unfairly and unintentionally underinsured.

• So you can still afford a vacation: Office visits can be covered to varying levels and in different ways.

The patient usually has to pay a deductible, an annual base, over which the company pays most or all charges. If it does not pay all charges, make sure that there is an upper limit on your share (usually 20 percent at the start). Try to insure yourself fully for the worst-case scenario and, if possible, use your own savings to self-insure smaller charges. Some people buy policies as though they are sure they'll always go through life getting colds, so to speak, but never pneumonia.

Lately, the fee-for-service health plans offered by indemnity companies have been shunted aside by the growing dominance of managed health care. The difference, echoing the description above, is that a managed plan takes care of the patient; the expenses are not racked up and then repaid, as in indemnity plans.

Health maintenance organizations (HMOs) started in California in the 1940s, but caught on nationwide in the 1970s, offering clients a version of the super-comprehensive medical care found in Europe and thought by many to be vastly superior to the prevailing chaos in the United States.

The HMOs actually tried to do something about the American system. They were clinics with long arms into the health-care system, and by insisting on cooperation throughout, they lowered costs. Clients were charged a yearly premium for complete care, including discounted medicines and an extremely low fee per office visit.

While traditional fee-for-service insurance companies tried to encourage frugal care from a skyscraper in another time zone—to the annoyance of good doctors and the amusement of unscrupulous ones—HMOs were right on site, smiling at patients and assuring them that everything was under control. What was mainly under control were doctors and the rest of the medical community.

Most Americans have medical insurance as an employee benefit. Even so, choices abound as never before. HMOs provide the least expensive protection for those who need regular care—families in particular. [The saving is sometimes passed along to employees.] However, HMOs do not allow patients much choice. Even for those who are unsentimental about continuing to see nice Dr. Washburn, there may be a time when only the best specialist in town will do. And the HMO may designate the second- or even twenty-second-best specialist in town. If such a scenario seems plausible, consider a *preferred provider organization,* a managed-care program that leaves the choice of doctor largely to the patient. Insurance companies are offering them to compete with HMOs, while HMOs are spawning them to compete with insurance companies. Hail the American chaos!

GOOD TO BE HOME

Anything that happens to your home happens to you, even if you are away. If someone has broken in, it isn't unusual for you to walk around and touch everything, just to pull it back from the realm of the stranger. And if the house is destroyed, there is a reason to rebuild that is stronger than the need for shelter. When the house is back, so is the spirit.

One of the two types of homeowner coverage is named *peril* insurance, by which you get to name those catastrophes against which you would like protection. The *all-risk policy,* on the other hand, will cover any strange occurrence, such as someone flushing a toilet in a plane at 35,000 feet and hitting your chimney with the accuracy of a stealth bomber. Civil war is not normally covered, so keep that in mind. And it is rather amusing to note that nuclear war is not covered either. Just in case you're visiting Tallahassee on the day the world is obliterated, no one will replace your stereo. More important, though, is that floods and earthquakes aren't covered in standard policies. Both have been around a lot longer than either you or your house, so it seems futile to hope that they couldn't occur in places where they are prevalent.

Residents of rental properties, condominiums, and co-op apartments need not worry about insuring the physical building in which they live; that is already covered. However, belongings must be covered, even if it is true that— as your best friend has often noted in a subtle way—your decor is just a lot of worthless junk. Homeowner policies also include liability coverage, in case someone sues you for injuries sustained on or for damages caused by your property. The standard coverage is for about $100,000, but you may want to ask your lawyer to suggest a more suitable figure, in light of special circumstances. You might hold big parties, for example, or keep a great white shark in the bathtub.

In any type of homeowner coverage, take care to insure the replacement value of the house or belongings, by one means or another. In the case of a structure, the market value has nothing to do with the replacement cost. Sometimes it's lower, sometimes higher. Have the replacement cost assessed every seven years or so, or else buy a policy that provides full replacement value. In the case of the objects and furniture, you are also well advised to opt for replacement-cost insurance in most cases. However, if you have many antiques and pieces of artwork, insure them for a specific amount, according to your knowledge of the market for such items (and update your policy as often as the market shifts). The insurance company may not otherwise recognize the full value of a seventeenth-century desk so magnificent that Chippendale copied *it*. They'll call it one medium desk, wood.

THE AUTO RACE

Driving laws are the same everywhere, or nearly so. Roads are about the same. Drivers are almost the same. Cars are the same. And lawyers are spread out fairly evenly. But auto insurance laws differ wildly.

Checklist

1. Find out what the insurance will cost before you buy a car. Insurance companies have an unfortunate prejudice against interesting vehicles, such as an expensive sportscar.

2. *Bodily injury liability coverage* should be steep ($300,000 at the least; $1 million is not unheard of) in case you accidentally badly hurt someone or kill someone. *Property liability* also covers you against lawsuits, but only for property ($75,000 would be very good coverage).

3. *Medical coverage* provides at least some level of care (about $5,000 per person) for those in your car, if they are hurt; health insurance may kick in instead, but then, everybody you cart around may not have health insurance.

4. *Collision insurance* pays for damage to your car. Try to have it written as replacement coverage or, if your car isn't worth much anyway, lower the coverage however you can and self-insure the risk of damage. (Don't necessarily let collision lapse altogether, since it may cover you as a driver in other circumstances.)

5. *Comprehensive* coverage pays for damage or loss to the car itself, including theft and fire.

6. *Uninsured motorist insurance* is vital, especially since some states do not require realistic levels of automobile insurance and even so, plenty of people are on the loose without any insurance at all. One of most horrifying articles that ever ran in *The New Yorker* magazine was the narrative of a woman in West Virginia whose husband was injured in an accident with an uninsured driver. Gripping though the two-part story was, it can be summed up in a sentence: Their lives were ruined and the uninsured motorist was utterly unaffected by the whole incident.

A POLICY OF TAKING OUT POLICIES

Another type of useful insurance is *liability insurance.* Now that lawsuits have become something of a legal lottery for people who have their lucky day when they break a fingernail on your doorknob, *umbrella liability* insurance has been developed as a form of protection that goes wherever you do. It can be written in any amount, but policies providing $1 million in coverage are typical and quite reasonable at a few hundred dollars a year.

A couple of policies that you may want, but don't need:

Flight insurance. People pay $10 to $15 for flight insurance, usually right at the airport, and if they are killed in a crash on the flight specified, the beneficiary will receive about $100,000. Credit card companies are now offering to dock your account for the same type of premium, every time you buy a plane ticket. How thoughtful! It is probably the most expensive of any policy extant, because it amounts to a few hours' worth of life insurance. Why do people sign up? It makes them feel less afraid. What to do instead? 1. If it makes you feel better, carry a photocopy of your life insurance policy in your pocket on plane trips. It will likely cover your beneficiaries for at least $100,000, should the plane—not crash (it's bad luck to say that)—just keep going up until it gets to Mars. 2. Check to see if by charging the plane ticket on one of your credit cards you are entitled to flight insurance at *no extra charge*. 3. Be a brave soldier.

Dread disease insurance. If you watch television for more than about eight minutes, read any of the magazines found within a yard of the grocery store cash register, or inadvertently eavesdrop on the average bus, it's bound to occur to you that you've got all the symptoms. All the symptoms, that's all. Of something bad. But what to do?

Dread disease coverage, a notably crude type of policy, covers a person for just one disease, chosen from a short list beginning with cancer. It may not even cover the complete treatment, but anyway, it is wildly inefficient as a form of health coverage. Why do people sign up? It makes them feel less afraid. What to do instead? 1. Verify that the Major Medical portion of your health coverage extends to at least $1 million over the course of your lifetime. 2. Walk around the block at least six times and brighten up before you get back. Health insurance is prudent, but dread disease insurance is just morbid. 3. Eat an apple a day.

SELECTED GLOSSARY

Cash value: In whole life insurance, the *surrender value* of a policy. The cash value reflects the amount of savings and interest that has accrued in the customer's name.

Deductible: The base amount that the holder of any type of policy will have to pay toward claims before the company begins payment. Always consider that premiums decrease dramatically for customers willing to take on a higher deductible.

First-to-die and Second-to-die policies: Life insurance policies that can be written to protect either member of a couple or of a business partnership. The first-to-die protects the surviving person directly; the second-to-die type of policy protects dependents in the event that both policyholders die.

Independent agent: An insurance agent who represents a variety of companies, rather than only one. The agent can thus help the customer find the most economical coverage.

No-fault: A type of policy that pays benefits without assigning blame. In automobile and other liability policies, some states have succeeded in lowering the cost of insurance by mandating that it doesn't matter who caused an accident; each company pays for the medical expenses of its own clients.

GET IN TOUCH

Health Care Financing Administration
6325 Security Blvd.
Baltimore, MD 21207
410–966–3000
Office of the federal government that will send brochures
with guidance on Medicare and Medicaid.

For insurance company ratings:

A.M. Best
A.M. Best Rd.
Oldwick, NJ 08858
908–439–2200; **www.ambest.com**
Sells ratings guides covering various aspects of the insurance business. Call 900–420–0400 for ratings on particular companies; a charge will be applied.

Standard & Poor's Insurance Ratings
25 Broadway
New York, NY 10004
212–438–2000; **www.standardandpoors.com**
Sells ratings guides; supplies free rating on any one individual company.

Insurance Consumer Help Line
800–942–4242
Hotline operated by the National Association of Life
Underwriters to answer questions and offer guidance on
complaints regarding all types of insurance.

United Seniors Health Cooperative
1331 H St., NW, Suite 500
Washington, DC 20005
202–393–6222
Provides material on health insurance and long-term care.

SIX ON THE WEB

www.consumerfed.org (Consumer Federation of America). Offers a life insurance evaluation, in addition to publications related to many other financial topics.

www.underwriter.com (Life Insurance Analysis Center). Calculates the amount of coverage needed.

www.iii.org (Insurance Information Institute). Offers background information and advice concerning all types of insurance: not merely buying policies, but getting the most out of them.

www.hiaa.org (Health Insurance Association of America). Consumer information on the complexities of health coverage, including projections for personal needs and news.

www.insure.com (Consumer Insurance Guide). More commercialized than it sounds, the site offers quotes on a full range of policies, along with news and tips.

www.annuitynet.com (Lincoln National Life Insurance Co.). Sells annuities and other long-term vehicles, but also offers considerable background on the subject, which is often overlooked in favor of flashier investments.

Chapter 5

INCOME TAX TIME

YOU MUST REMEMBER THIS

You already know what you must remember. Income taxes have grown to be much too complicated. The most effective ways to save money usually require several years' planning. The most effective ways to save time depend on detailed record keeping. . . . Paid tax preparers range from those who can simply fill out a return to those who can project long-range strategies. In any case, a client should be sure that the return is double-checked by someone else in the same office that prepared it. . . . The Internal Revenue Service is the best source for up-to-date information, but get their comments in writing.

Some people don't know who the president is. Some don't know where Delaware is. Some who live in Delaware don't know where Delaware is. However, except for a small handful of people, all Americans do taxes. They buckle down and begin with filing status, struggle through adjusted gross income, and advance to earned income credit payments, before persevering all the way to the suspense at the end: "if line 51 is more than line 58, subtract line 58 from . . ." They *learn the difference* between cost and accrual. And for only one reason. Their country, the land they love, is nuts. It can't simply take its citizens by the throat, shove splinters into their fingernails, and demand coins, like any decent tyrant of the thirteenth century. No, never. It makes them sit down at the kitchen table for a whole spring weekend and account. Cruel and unusual punishment is explicitly banished in a noble phrase, but not the words, "If required, attach Schedule D." It is the ultimate loyalty test, but practically everyone muddles through it, somehow. Americans must love their country, that is for sure. Some future day, a tyrant will wave a cracked and yellowed Form 1040 before a mob and threaten to use it if they don't calm down.

1913

The current income tax law was instituted in 1913, when the rates were carefully calculated to equal the thin end of a wedge, or about 1 percent. Four years later, the country had to face up to its role in World War I, and the tax nudged up somewhat. The high rate was 63 percent on an income of $1 million or more. Five years earlier, Mary Pickford, and anyone else making that kind of money, could have kept it all; in 1917, she would have had to hand in more than $600,000—about a week's salary for her.

After that, the income tax became a veritable natural resource for the country, a highly renewable one that created bustling new industries: battalions of lobbyists working to change the law; agents seeking to enforce it; accountants and preparers trying to make it viable.

In the Middle Ages, heads of state and churches started cathedral projects, which generated work spanning hundreds of years. The cathedrals were elaborate, national sculptures crawling with experts and craftsmen. America's equivalent is the income tax system, a cathedral of sorts, in intricacy, and one suited to its own century in keeping a whole body of white-collar craftspeople working in perpetuity.

THE TAX MAN

The general philosophy of the income tax is that personal expenditures that could ultimately help America are not taxed. Either the country figures it is ultimately saving itself money by allowing certain deductions, such as those for health care, or it plans on reaping future generations of taxable activity by allowing others, such as business-related expenses. The majority of income tax rules amount to a system of incentives that encourage or reward some activities and discourage others in the interest of a stable society. Someday, perhaps everyone will finally acquiesce and lead the exact same life. Until then, the forms have to be as complicated as the myriad people who have to fill them out.

If a sketch of the Perfect American were rendered, as described by income tax forms, it would start in the broad strokes of the 1040. The Perfect American is married to a person who doesn't make much money. Together, they have children who are quite a lot cheaper by the dozen (at a few thousand each). They own a home, and it is mortgaged to the hilt. The Perfect American works for someone else. The Perfect American never gets sick, saves assiduously for old age, and loses money on all of his or her investments.

Rather Taxing

According to the Internal Revenue Service, the estimated average time to complete a 1040 is almost 11 hours. About 200 million of the forms are filed each year, meaning that something like 92 million days are devoted to filling out the 1040.

That doesn't count the time devoted to the Schedules, A through E or SE (short). Nonetheless, 92 million days all by itself is equal to 25,000 years.

Each year, 25,000 years are spent filling out the 1040.

A country could build a lot of cathedrals in 25,000 years. This chapter can't keep up with continuing changes or new rulings in the tax code. It can't give accurate, specific advice. The IRS can't even give accurate, specific advice 7 percent of the time. Its accuracy rate for questions posed by taxpayers is 93 percent. However, in the interest of saving the United States in general and you in particular a few thousand years, this chapter is devoted to tax ideas. For quick reference, it is in the form of one long list, divided into topics. If each idea saved just one million days . . .

RETURN FARE: FIFTY IDEAS

A tax tip might be construed as advice, and there is no advice on taxes applicable to 200 million people at one time. Well, perhaps there is but it would be fairly basic.

Tax Tips for Everyone

1. **A good sign.** Sign the check; the IRS can charge interest or even a late payment penalty otherwise.

2. **And sign the forms.** That's not just another reminder, but a responsibility in cases wherein a paid preparer filled out the forms. Look them over carefully nonetheless, because it's still your form.

3. **A file duffle.** Keeping organized files of receipts is the best method you can use for record keeping. Banking or tax-related computer programs will help to track deductions throughout the year, but the paper in hand is still important. Even a duffle will do if it keeps receipts from being lost or thrown out.

Avoiding the Hornet

A few flags that may bring on an audit include:

4. **Ciphering.** The IRS can add. Whatever the numbers may be, go through the return one last time and make sure it all jibes.

5. **Sainthood.** If you give an inordinate amount to charity, obtain and keep receipts. You should have a canceled check or receipt for donations under $250, and a detailed receipt for those over that amount.

6. **Deducting the den.** The very sight of a deduction for use of a room at home for business will raise suspicions, so don't claim a deduction for devoting part of your home for business unless it is practically unusable for anything else.

7. **The great provider.** Claiming more than one or two

dependents over the age of eighteen may trigger an investigation.

8. **Matchmaking.** Copy numbers exactly from all forms sent by banks or investment companies. If the bank tells the IRS that it paid you $342 in interest and you write down that the bank gave you $324, the discrepancy may jiggle your return into the pile marked for inquiry. Don't skip any germane amounts, even tiny ones, as the IRS takes any hint of unreported income as a personal affront.

9. **Consistency.** Refer to last year's returns and make sure that you have not inadvertently changed any descriptive codes—for example, the principal business code on Schedule C (profit or loss).

Capital Gains

Sharing the wealth.

10. **Keep the cash.** If you have stock or other property that has appreciated so that it is subject to a capital-gains tax, give it to charity in lieu of an intended cash donation.

11. **Little guys.** Stocks held in qualifying small companies for more than five years have a special exclusion that cuts the capital gain in half.

Tax Freebies

12. **Paul Munis.** The interest income from a "muni," or municipal bond, is not subject to federal tax. Municipal bonds are issued by villages, states, school districts, or even . . . municipalities. They help to finance large proj-

ects, such as road building. Some munis are not subject to state or local taxes, either. The income is subject to self-employment tax, however.

13. **Graduating interest.** The interest on Series EE U.S. savings bonds is not taxed when used directly for college tuition (see Chapter 1).

14. **Free quarters.** Some publicly traded companies pay a tax-free dividend.

15. **Stock up now.** Dividends in the form of stock usually do not count as taxable income.

Working Down the Taxes

The following are job-related benefits that aren't taxed as income; let the employer pay you to the hilt through these means rather than with cash. If, that is, you plan to spend money in these areas anyway.

16. **Hale and hearty.** Medical and disability insurance premiums paid by an employer are not taxed as income.

17. **A little life.** If the employer pays for group term life insurance with a death benefit of $50,000 or less, it is tax free.

18. **Pure class.** If the employer pays college tuition, it is not taxed as additional income up to a certain amount of several thousand dollars.

19. **Deferring down the taxes.** Some or all of the employer's contribution to pensions, and IRAs in some cases, are untaxed at the time they are made.

Timing

20. **Your ship has finally docked.** If you make inordinately more money one year than you will the next, you can have the employer defer the income. You cannot, however, hide the income by merely failing to cash a check until the following year.

21. **New Year's Eve.** Make major charitable donations in December. That way you can have the use of the money all year and yet still have a deduction.

22. **How to file April 16.** If you foresee that you will be late in filling out your forms, send in Form 4868, a fairly simple one for an automatic four-month extension on filing, but *not* on paying. With a 10 percent leeway, your taxes are still due by April 15.

23. **Declarations.** Under some circumstances, you may pay less on the capital gain realized from a stock than on dividend income from it. If you are thinking of selling anyway, try to do so when the stock is ex-dividend, so that the dividend-plus is in the price and will be counted as part of the gain.

24. **Happy New Year.** You can make a qualifying contribution to an IRA (Individual Retirement Account) until April 15 of the year following the one for which you are filing. If you swear you are not forgetful or sloppy, you can even claim an IRA deduction that hasn't been made yet on a return filed in January. After you receive your refund in March or so, you can then use *it* in order to make the stipulated deposit in the IRA. It's shenanigans, but legal, so long as you follow through.

Staδheδ

Taxes need not be paid now on income properly ear-marked.

25. **Set it aside.** IRAs can be opened at banks, broker-ages, and other institutions by people who don't have a retirement account where they work, and by certain others. You can siphon several thousand dollars per year out of your income and pay the taxes on it after you are fifty-nine and before you are seventy.

26. **HR-10 plans.** Better known as Keogh plans, HR-10s are tax-deferred accounts that can be opened by peo-ple who are self-employed. You can set aside much more money each year than you could in an IRA. (There is more on these and other tax-deferred plans in Chapter 8 on long-term planning.)

Nitpickδ

Scrubbing every penny off the tax bill.

27. **Brother, can you spare a receipt?** Get a receipt for every donation of old clothes, food at a food drive, casual cash donation, and baked goodies for a sale.

28. **Sick leave.** Medical expenses totaling more than 7.5 percent of your income are deductible. If you have some expenses approaching that amount, and need any optional dental or physical treatment, try to schedule it all in the same year to bump the total over the threshold.

Records

29. **In the glove compartment.** Keep a little notebook in the car all year long to record odometer readings, total mileage, date, destination, and incidental expenses for all trips related to taxable activity. Always take toll and gas receipts as corroboration of mileage records.

30. **Bank statements.** Financial institutions will send year-end statements, but don't throw out the monthly ones.

31. **Brokerage statements.** Capital-gains rules require extensive record keeping. To fill out pertinent schedules, you will need exact dates and other readings not normally included on year-end statements. Don't throw out individual confirmations.

32. **Big closets.** Keep all your records for six years in case of an audit. Keep tax return forms and major receipts forever.

Odds and Ends

33. **Get it in writing.** The IRS will answer taxpayer questions over the telephone or in person at field offices. Obtain anything but the most basic advice in writing; other than that, you may be responsible for penalties arising even from agent misinformation.

34. **Exact estimate.** People who are not having enough taxes withheld to cover their tax bill to within $500 (or at least 90 percent of the bill) must make estimated payments throughout the year. The estimated taxes must reflect at least 90 percent of the tax actually computed the following April. If they fall short, there still may

not be a penalty as long as the estimate reflects at least 100 percent of the previous year's actual tax (110 percent if your adjusted gross income was more than $150,000).

35. **Haste and waste.** Tax preparation firms that offer to advance you the amount of your refund usually charge exorbitant interest; don't pay out any more at tax time than you already have.

36. **Zap.** You can request a quicksilver, electronic refund that goes right into your bank account by filling out IRS Form 8888.

37. **Congeniality award.** If business is discussed over a meal or drinks served at home, the associated costs are deductible. Notes and receipts should indicate the guests and what general business subjects were discussed.

38. **One big party.** Half the cost of a skybox at a sporting event is deductible, if business associates were entertained at one game only. When the business uses a skybox for more than one game in a year, however, the deduction is for half the cost of nonskybox seats that would have accommodated the same number of guests.

Deductions That May Sneak Up

If you itemize . . .

39. **The cost of tax-deferred.** The fees associated with opening an IRA account can be deducted. Don't have the fees withdrawn from the account. Pay for them outright and get a receipt.

40. **Charity begins in the car.** You can deduct the mileage you rack up just to get to charity work.

41. **Make book.** Someday, it may happen. You may

win so much at the casino that the cashier has to report it
to the IRS. However, losses in the same year can be deducted against those winnings. Just in case, keep a jour-
nal of your gambling activity: dates, amount risked,
amount on hand upon leaving. Checks cashed at the casino may also help to justify deductions for losses, although for reasons of self-control, you may not want to
initiate check-cashing privileges at a casino. The same
holds true for lottery winnings; losing tickets can be the
basis for deductions from winnings.

42. **Make work.** Deduct money you spend to get a
new job, so long as it is largely the same kind of job you
have now. Farmers can't suddenly become baritones.
Well, they can, but they can't deduct the voice lessons.

43. **Make fun.** If you have a hobby that generates a
small income, you can deduct costs up to the amount of
the income.

44. **Joiners.** Professional memberships and subscrip-
tions can be deductible. Courses or seminars taken to
maintain your proficiency in your job may be deductible,
although the IRS is touchy about it. To hazard an expla-
nation, you can't deduct courses that make you better at
your job, only ones that help you hang in there at the
same level.

45. **Jobbers.** Expenses incurred to keep meetings with
clients are deductible. Keep receipts for taxi fare or other
transportation expenses.

46. **And they better tell you this.** Fees paid to tax
preparers are deductible, as are any charges for anyone
who electronically files the return for you.

A Rough Buck

47. **Grateful nation.** If you join the U.S. Army and serve in a hazardous zone, your pay is tax free.

48. **Deducted.** If your home was burglarized and if you can prove it and if you have receipts for the items stolen and if you received no insurance money and if the loss is not too awfully great, then the IRS will endeavor to cheer you up by giving you a deduction.

Income Reductions

. . . even if you don't itemize.

49. **Bad seeds.** A bad debt can be claimed for the year in which it became irretrievable.

50. **Family obligations.** Taxpayers who jointly take care of an otherwise destitute relative can alternate in claiming that person as a dependent.

DRAMA RETURNS

People who don't pay income taxes go to jail.

No, that's not right. People who don't file income tax *returns* go to jail. Whether or not a person has taxes due is another matter. But the Internal Revenue Service wants a return from practically everybody. It is much more likely to forgive nonreturners who come forward and repent than scoundrels it has to catch.

Minimum earnings levels, depending on the source, change every year and apply differently to people in particular situations at various stages (an IRS sentence, if ever there was one). Allowing for generalization, anyone who has seen serious money in the past year should look into the regulation. Children (under fourteen) have to pay tax on income of a little more than a thousand dollars and up.

HELP THAT DOESN'T HURT

Taxpayers in our time, described by their ideal experiences:

Profile 1. Stop at the tax service, drop off a wrinkled manila envelope full of paystubs and statements. Go out to the club and play eighteen. Return for the return. Presto! Total time spent on taxes: eight minutes.

Profile 2. Keep neat files of excellent records all year long. Net result: neat files full of questions. Make an appointment at tax time for a three-hour consultation with a professional, who may just surprise and amaze with savings from unexpected quarters. Total time spent on taxes: fifteen hours (ten throughout the year, and five at tax time).

Profile 3. Schedule meetings every three months with the tax professional to discuss imminent changes in personal finances and project five or more years into the future, while maintaining contact between said tax professional and financial planner, broker, or other interested parties. Total time spent on taxes: about a half hour . . . out of every hour.

Five types of assistance are available, corresponding only roughly to the profiles above. The *commercial preparer* is a person. That is all you can be sure of, just from the designation. Commercial preparers are usually bookkeepers, accountants, or teachers who take the seasonal work of filling in forms at storefront tax-preparation offices. If you go to a storefront, make sure you know where the people behind the operation can be found after tax season. The charge for a fairly simple return should be less than $75; if your return requires more than $200 worth of service, it also requires a preparer with a higher certification. The *enrolled agent,* who may well work at a storefront office, is either a former IRS auditor or has passed an IRS test for competency. The IRS will recognize the enrolled agent in any dispute. As a proportional description, based on the fee named above, the charge for a fairly simple return will be more like $125.

A *public accountant* is a designation subject to state board certification. Public accountants are trained in tax matters, but the IRS does not recognize them officially. *Certified public accountants* (CPAs) are on a par with lawyers within the field of accounting. They are college educated and stringently vetted by state boards. However, in actual practice, a CPA is not necessarily any more savvy than a public accountant. Both deal routinely with tax matters and some are better than others. The CPA is, however, allowed to represent clients before the IRS, as is the tax attorney. The *tax attorney,* a specialist on matters of taxation, is paid to see the bigger picture—whatever bigger picture you are trying to paint.

One characteristic is missing from the various taxpayer profiles: total income. It is an error to assume that people of lower income don't need expert advice. The factors in question are the complexity of the return in any one year and the need for specialized planning. The right level of assistance doesn't indicate income, but it can certainly help preserve it.

Checklist for selecting help:

1. Find out the preparer's level of experience with returns or special situations you may have.

2. Agree on a fee in advance; make it either flat or hourly, but don't pay on a commission basis.

3. Make sure you know where the preparer will be after tax time in case a problem arises.

4. Ask the preparer for a list of the materials you should bring.

5. A tax return should be double-checked by someone else in the same office as part of the price.

One other profile not mentioned above, a Profile 4, prepares his or her own return, muddling through with no help at all, except for the kids or the dogs who jump on the bed and throw all the little piles of receipts and statements into a storm cloud that lands on the carpet. Somehow, that can work, too.

In addition, increasingly popular computer programs can take filers through every step of the income tax process in plain black and white. With income tax, though, the trouble spots are often spelled out in gray and grayer. While the CD-ROMs on the market are helpful with many of the complexities of the accounting, you still have to handle interpretations therein. The programs are best for people who have been filling out their own forms for years and who can spot glitches from their own experience. In lieu of hired tax preparation, the programs are also excellent for people with simple returns.

Giving a rough estimate, a tax bill can probably be reduced by 10 percent as the result of an expertly prepared return. But it can probably be reduced by a third with advance planning and relatively simple shifts in money management. No decision in your life should be made purely on the basis of decreasing your income tax, but informed choices over the years will always beat last-minute dashes through the tax code in search of loopholes. No matter what your income, you should project your tax-related activities for at least five years into the future. Have no fear; there will still be an income tax, and an April 15, that far down any road.

SELECTED GLOSSARY

Alternative minimum tax (AMT): Income tax computed on a different basis than the regular tax. Intended as a loophole closer, the AMT applies to returns on which the effect of certain types of investment has inordinately reduced the amount owed.

Capital gains: Profits! More specifically, profits realized from the sale of investments. *Capital losses* are the opposite.

Credit: In income tax terms, an amount subtracted outright from the tax total.

Depreciation: Expenses in the acquisition of property taken as a series of deductions spread out over a number of years, reflecting the natural decrease in the value of the article. *Straight-line depreciation* is an even projection, whereas *accelerated depreciation* allows bigger write-offs early on for some articles.

Estate tax: The tax on estates worth more than $600,000.

Gift tax: The tax applied to the amount over $10,000 given to each recipient.

Kiddie tax: The tax on a child's income in excess of $1,300, payable at the rate of the parent, and filed with Form 8615.

Tax shelter: A way to park cash out of the reach of the IRS, temporarily. Tax-deferred accounts are tax shelters, but the term usually applies to special investments that the government encourages by giving them some level of tax deferral or exemption. Such investments are, for example, for the exploration of natural resources or for the construction of low-income housing.

GET IN TOUCH

The IRS information center nearest you is listed in the telephone book, or you can call 800–829–1040. You can speak to an agent or ask for any one of hundreds of publications.

The IRS offers TeleTopics, which are clearly written explanations of about 150 subjects, available via fax by calling 703–487–4160. The complete list of TeleTopics is included in the annual tax booklet sent to every taxpayer. Here are a dozen of the more popular titles: 101, IRS Services; 201, What to Do if You Can't Pay Your Tax; 254, How to Choose a Tax Preparer; 302, Highlights of Tax Changes; 354, Dependents; 407, Business Income; 420, Bartering Income; 452, Alimony Paid; 502, Medical and Dental Expenses; 511, Business Travel Expenses; 554, Self-Employment tax; 701, Sale of Your Home.

National Association of Enrolled Agents
6000 Executive Blvd., Suite 205
Rockville, MD 20852
800–424–4339
Help in finding an enrolled agent to engage as a tax preparer.

SIX ON THE WEB

www.irs.ustreas.gov/prod/cover.html (Internal Revenue Service). Lists forms and instructions, publications, and daily tax news.

www.taxweb.com (Webtech Consulting, Inc.). Detailed information for the taxpayer, including calendar of filing dates, information on refunds, enforcement, state tax, and so on. Also includes links.

www.tax.org (Tax Analysts Online). As the name implies, this is a more analytical site, with a thoughtful, ongoing discussion of taxation and its implications for both the filer and the government.

www.nolo.com (Nolo Press). Billing itself as the Self-help Law Center, this is a cheerfully presented encyclopedia of law topics ranging from divorce to real estate, but dealing extensively with tax issues.

www.rothira.com (Roth IRA). Contains up-to-date articles on the uses of the Roth-IRA.

www.fairmark.com (Fairmark Press Tax Guide). Directed at investors, Fairmark's site covers such topics as capital gains, custodial accounts, and mutual funds.

Chapter 6

SPENDING MONEY

YOU MUST REMEMBER THIS

Our nation encourages spending at every turn, so many households lose sight of their individual priorities in making purchases. . . . Budgets can either be strict, figured down to the penny, or coercive, intended to alter habitual problem areas in spending. . . . For all the money saved by shopping sales and using coupons, hidden costs and seemingly small fees in a wide range can quietly add up to much more in lost money.

The issue of spending money is far, far removed from that of necessity or even of quality of life. Some people buy all the latest junk. Some buy absurdly high-style, or overtly low-style, junk. Some buy sensible junk, but even that says something about the modern way of life; it is still buying. And so it is hard to know which are important purchases, really, and which can be chalked up to a nearly universal sentiment: It feels good to spend money and it looks good to spend money.

Keeping to a budget is similar to staying on a diet. It is impossible to stop either one completely—spending money or eating. In the first place, nothing is more instantly gratifying to the soul than blowing a budget, or a diet. And secondly, nothing is more instantly depressing than having blown it. For all the pressures acting on purchases, there seem to be two characteristics to avoid in trying to spend money wisely. One is being American. The other is being human.

INTERLOCKING RINGS

The asset ring discussed in Chapter 1 emerges generally from the household budget. The day-to-day balance of income and expenditure has to furnish an extra cushion, which can move into the asset ring. Or, cuing Charles Dickens in:

> Annual income 20 pounds, annual expenditure, 19 pounds; result: happiness. Annual income, 19 pounds; annual expenditure 20 pounds; result: misery.

Household budgets vary widely, just as households do. The basic goals for any of them, however, do not vary:

1. To provide needs and comforts proportionally (some people have a new CD player but can't afford a warm winter coat, not by choice but by haphazard planning).

2. To leave a comfortable amount for long-term savings or other uses in the asset ring.

Above all else, a budget has to be comfortable; it won't last long otherwise. In fact, the very word *budget* has a stringency about it, and so *expenditure ring* would actually be more accurate: something to be built, not fought.

SAMPLE EXPENDITURE RING	PER MONTH AT . . .		
	$20,000	$50,000*	$100,000*
For a single person:			
24% Housing (incl. rent or mortgage, utilities, regular maintenance)	$400	$1,000	$2,000
17.5% Taxes	$292	$1,042 (25%)	$2,292 (27.5%)
12.5% Car (incl. other transportation, parking)	$208	$521	$833 (10%)
3.5% Insurance	$58	$146	$292
5% Clothes	$83	$208	$417
10% Food	$167	$208 (5%)	$208 (2.5%)
9.5% Entertainment (incl. vacation, restaurants, hobbies)	$158	$396	$792
10% Savings	$167	$417	$1042 (12.5%)
8% Miscellaneous: (incl. medical/veterinary, education, debt service telephone, haircuts and cosmetics, charity)	$134	$229 (5.5%)	$458 (5.5%)
Total expenditures:	$1,667	$4,167	$8,334

*Note: figures in parentheses reflect adjustments in budget percentage, owing to higher incomes.

SAMPLE EXPENDITURE RING	PER MONTH AT . . .		
	$20,000	$50,000	$100,000
For a family of four: 25% Housing (incl. rent or mortgage, utilities, regular maintenance)	$417	$1,042	$1,583 (19%)
16% Taxes	$267	$875 (21%)	$2,167 (26%)
13% Car(s) (incl. other transportation, parking)	$217	$500 (12%)	$833 (10%)
7% Insurance	$117	$250 (6%)	$500 (6%)
8% Clothes	$133	$292 (7%)	$417 (5%)
15% Food	$250	$375 (9%)	$500 (6%)
5% Entertainment (incl. vacation, restaurants, hobbies)	$83	$250 (6%)	$583 (7%)
7% Savings	$117	$375 (9%)	$1,083 (13%)
4% Miscellaneous: (incl. medical/veterinary, education, debt service, telephone, haircuts and cosmetics, charity)	$67	$208 (5%)	$667 (8%)
Total expenditures:	$1,667	$4,167	$8,334

SAMPLE EXPENDITURE RING

	PER MONTH AT . . .		
	$20,000	$50,000	$100,000
For a couple near retirement:			
20% Housing (incl. rent or mortgage, utilities, regular maintenance)	$333	$708 (17%)	$1,250 (15%)
18% Taxes	$300	$917 (22%)	$2,291 (25%)
12% Car (incl. other transportation, parking)	$200	$458 (11%)	$750 (9%)
3% Insurance	$50	$125	$333 (4%)
5% Clothes	$83	$208	$333 (4%)
10% Food	$167	$333 (8%)	$417 (5%)
10% Entertainment (incl. vacation, restaurants, hobbies)	$167	$458 (11%)	$1,000 (12%)
12% Savings	$200	$583 (14%)	$1,500 (18%)
10% Miscellaneous: (incl. medical/veterinary, education, debt service, telephone, haircuts and cosmetics, charity)	$167	$375 (9%)	$667 (8%)
Total expenditures	$1,667	$4,167	$8,334

How to start construction. The first step in building your own expenditure ring is to . . . do nothing. Don't change your spending habits or try to; just write down what you spend for three or four weeks. Use the columns above at first, and then alter them into specifics that suit your habits. At first, you can throw anything you want into the miscellaneous column, but after a month or so, that percentage should flatten out to a low amount. Depending on your habits, you will probably break food and restaurants down into weekly amounts, whereas insurance and vacation costs may be easier to budget on an annual basis.

Computers can be helpful in maintaining an expenditure ring, making all record keeping available for banking or tax files. Do whatever you need to, though, to learn the mechanism of your own expenditure. The following is a sample:

ACTUAL EXPENDITURE RING	ANTICIPATED PERCENTAGE	ANTICIPATED AMOUNT	ACTUAL AMOUNT	NOTES
Weeks 8–12				
Housing:	26%	$544	$525	
rent		$487	$487	
electricity		$47	$38	+$9
repairs		$10	zero	+$10
Taxes (withholding)	18%	$383	$383	
Car (owned outright)	13%	$297	$269	
parking		$197	$197	
gas, oil, repairs		$100	$72	+$28
Insurance	7%	$141	$141	
home		$33	$33	
car		$62	$62	
health		$46	$46	
Clothes	1%	$25	$22	+$3
Food	4%	$75	$94	−$19
Entertainment	1%	$20	$32	−$12
Vacation	2.5%	$50	zero	+$50
Restaurants	2.5%	$50	$100	−$50
Horseback riding	2.5%	$50	$100	−$50
Savings	9.5%	$200	$200	
Medical/veterinary	2%	$40	$24	+$16
Telephone	5.5%	$110	$140	−$30
Charity	1%	$20	zero	+$20
Gifts	2.5%	$50	$50	
Sundries	1%	$25	$25	
Miscellaneous	1%	$25	$100	−$75
		2,105 = 25,260 mo. year	2,205 = 26,580 mo. year	

In the expenditure ring above, the ringleader has gone over the monthly budget by $100 and will have to decide where the problems lie, with an eye to making up the shortfall in the following month. Note that money that is under- or overspent is tracked in the last column. Some expenses, such as car repairs, occur only occasionally, one always hopes, and so the budgeted money can stay in reserve in those categories. However, the expenditure ring should be readjusted from time to time, so that excess reserves can be shifted and the percentages tuned up.

AUTOMATIC BUDGETING DEVICES

1. **Impulse attack.** Make it your steadfast rule never to buy anything over $50 (or $100) without thinking it over for a day. Deflect both the wiles of the salesperson and your own flush of enthusiasm with the same sentiment, "I never buy anything without sleeping on it first." Half the time you'll wake up practically limp with relief that you didn't take the plunge, and half the time you'll go back and make the purchase. Either way, no harm done.

2. **Shop at home.** Some crackerjack shoppers don't buy anything that isn't on their list, which is compiled at home, where they can make all their shopping decisions soberly.

3. **Branded.** Before buying almost anything, give it this test: "If I knew with certainty that people would never see me with this thing I am getting, would I still get it?" You may genuinely want a Bentley convertible or a Rolex watch. Or you may be seeking respect through such items. It's helpful to know the difference before you take the plunge.

4. **Use real money.** Nearly everyone spends more when using a credit card than when using cash. If you want to put the brakes on outflow, use cash habitually. A credit card may return a 1 or 2 percent on your purchases just to give you a glow of frugality every time you use it. However, the odds are good that, overall, you spend 10 to 30 percent more with credit cards than you would with cash. Most people do.

5. **Restaurants are expensive.** They are also a way of life, and there are many people who could actually live in nicer housing if they didn't eat out so much. But they like

to eat out. However, if you are trying to save money, recognize that except for single people eating in cheap places (perchance to be painted by Edward Hopper), restaurants waste your money. Frozen entrees (which is what a lot of restaurants serve, anyway) and drinks from the store cost on average a fifth of what is charged at a restaurant. Food made from scratch costs more like a tenth. In round numbers, a dollar's worth of hamburger costs about $30 at the 21 Club in New York, but then, they coax it into pretty good shape for the price. In other words, restaurants can be great whatever the cost. On a budget, however, set a low limit on how many times per week you indulge.

6. **Rockefeller's tip.** John D. Rockefeller extolled his own tip for saving money: He kept a small notebook of all expenditures. Nothing worked better, he maintained, in training a person to keep from frittering away money than simply knowing where it went.

AT HOME WITH CHEAPSKATES
BILL AND PENNY POUNDLY

Bill: Hey! Don't park in the driveway. Your car might leak and we're not repaving for three years, two months, and thirteen days. *[Waits.]* Now, over here, this is our ten-year-old Volvo. It still runs well, but at that age, it's not worth insuring with either comprehensive or collision, and we save on that. We put a lot of money in the tires, because they improve gas mileage and safety. We paid $2,000 for the car and put $1,000 into it in repairs, so we do not foresee any major expenditures. In addition, we chose this one because it's gray, the color least likely to fade and need to be repainted.

Us: You probably get a lot of attention with that car at the beach.

Penny: Walk through the garage. We use a hand-reel lawn mower. It cost $90 and doesn't need gas, oil, or spring tune-ups. It does a fine job on the grass, and it doesn't pollute. We cut our homeowner policy by 5 percent just by making sure that our agent was aware of the qualifying safety equipment we have: fire extinguishers, smoke alarms, dead-bolt locks, and locks for all the windows. The total outlay was about $150.

Bill: A full-service alarm system would take about 10 percent off the premium, in addition. We are just not yet sure we want to take that step, for the expense and inconvenience. Also, we're just not sure it's necessary. By the way, it's a pretty ugly house, isn't it?

Us: Well, you sure don't see many like it.

Bill: Built by a mad Moravian bricklayer. Brick houses cost less to insure. By the way, we planted maples on the east and west sides of our house to block the wind, make shade, and generally keep the air around the house insulated. We didn't want any species too short or thick. That would give thieves a protective curtain. Anyway, the bigger those trees grow, the more we see it in our heat and air-conditioning bill. Someday, we ought to be able to see our AC usage cut to half of what it was when we moved in, thanks to those maples.

Penny: Come on in. We found that the cost of adding this breezeway would be met by further savings in our heat and air-conditioning bills, in just under ten years.

Bill: We try to run most of our major appliances late at night, when the cost of electricity is a fifth of what it is during the day. Some of them, like the dishwasher, even have timers.

Penny: Would you like something to drink?

Us: Sure, what do you have?

Bill: Water. We save money on food in most of the usual ways, clipping coupons, stocking up on specials, and going to the farmer's market as much as possible, but we also save a lot by substituting. We make popcorn ourselves instead of buying snack food.

Penny: We don't buy salad in bags. We make it ourselves every few days and put it in airtight bags.

Bill: We grate our own cheese.

Penny: We're eating hot cereal these days, because it's less expensive than most of the cold kinds.

Us: I get it.

Penny: We set a budget and we've just found ways to stay within it.

Bill: Come on upstairs. When I get home from work, if I hang my suits right up and make sure that air can circulate around them, I don't have to go to the dry cleaners as often. And I launder my own shirts. I iron them while I watch golf on Sunday afternoons. You know, it actually makes the golf more exciting to iron all the while.

Us: I can believe that.

Penny: Shoe trees and cream, not polish, double the life of our shoes.

Us: But it's easy for you to save money. You don't have any children.

Penny: Sure, we do. We have three, thirteen to seventeen. We spoil them rotten.

Bill: We sure do.

Penny: We let them spend half the money they earn absolutely any way they want. How's that for generous?

Us: And you keep the rest to put toward popcorn?

Penny: We put it aside for their college tuition.

Bill: We're cheapskates for a reason, you know.

Hot Fritters

A Philosophical Quizlet: If Glynis goes to a great deal of trouble to save a dollar here, and then lets it go utterly to waste there, what is the net effect?

A. It is a wash at zero: plus one dollar and minus one?

B. Did she gain a buck by saving, after all, considering that she could have been at minus two, otherwise?

C. Did she lose a dollar by her frittering, considering that she could have been at plus two, with more discipline?

All the answers are correct—it being a philosophical quizlet—but your selection reflects a great deal about you and your ways with spending. If you answered A, you are probably running around in circles, where saving is concerned, but you're having a good time at it (half the time, anyway). If you answered B, you are a hopeless optimist, probably spending the same $10 six times before it is finally gone, and the only surprising thing is that you have gotten this far into any chapter on budgeting. Here's a pat on the back. If you answered C, you win. You are a rather gray little cloud and hard on yourself, but at least you have the right idea, which is that the only way to get ahead is to stay ahead.

All the C people undoubtedly know the following already, but the rest can learn a few practical tips on how *not* to fritter away money.

TROUBLE SPOTS FOR
THE MODERN BUDGET

If credit card debt has grown out-of-bounds, consolidate all accounts into one that has a low annual percentage rate. Do not use credit cards any further, and pay off the balance as soon as possible. If there is a chance in the world of bouncing a check that you need to write, use a credit card check instead (if they are available to you). They carry fees and interest charges, but even those are preferable to what banks will charge for "insufficient funds." Mind the ATM fees and arrange to cash checks at a store.

The average American household spends more than $1,000 per year on gambling, which is quite a big hole in

some sadly small pockets. Much of it goes to state governments, which apparently see nothing sad about it. Here is
one statistical fact to bear in mind: You are not going to
win the lottery. Not even if you throw your whole house
at it, which some people have done. Considering that this
is a book about personal finance, that statistic is true
enough. Budget for all gambling very strictly.

In traveling, always ask any reservations clerk or agent
what the cheapest fare is, even before you give any dates
or other preferences; you can be flexible if you know the
parameters. If the fare goes down after you buy a ticket,
you are entitled to a refund of the difference, but it may
be up to you to check the fare and ask for the difference.
Hotel room rates are often up for negotiation, especially
for late- or off-season bookings. Call the hotel directly, as
opposed to using a central booking office, and simply ask
for a better price. Ask what the corporate rate is; most
hotels will grant you that, if only as a reward for not lying
about being on company business in the first place. Call
state or local tourist boards in advance to receive free
maps and special offers concerning your destination. For
fast food on the road, you will probably get more for your
money at grocery stores, delis, and salad bars than at
restaurants.

It is not only best to buy groceries on a full stomach so
as not to reach for everything that looks good; it is important to eat a good meal before going to the movies or to a
ballpark. A single french fry or a microscopic soda can
cost more than the admission ticket. Buying holiday items
off-season is an obvious way for those with patience to
save money. However, as to gardens, many seeds that go
for clearance prices at the end of the summer can be

planted in the fall and will grow quite happily the following spring, in their own time.

Frugal people keep their refrigerators as empty as possible; not only does it save substantially on energy costs but it is also a fact that less food turns green and moldy if it can be seen and consumed than if it is buried behind the cream cheese and forgotten. Pets do not have to know that canned food exists, and then they will be happy with the less-expensive dry food. Once they find out, however—especially cats—you will have no choice in the matter, ever after.

Gifts can become a wicked sort of pyramid scheme, in which you give and give and give (this is the whole scheme) and give and give and—but why be petty? The important thing is to show you care: that they didn't get you anything last year. However, ruffled feathers aside, there are ways to save money on gifts, including, for example, giving a framed photo of the recipient looking good. Everybody wants to be seen looking good. You can also bake something delectable, which, in this day and age, is more welcome than a gigantic box from Cartier. That part is true, but then everybody knows that it's the little boxes from jewelry stores that count.

Rent-to-Own

People with very little money and no credit can have furniture or appliances under long-term agreements with a nominal purchase price. Known as rent-to-own, this practice is currently being questioned in the courts as a de facto credit plan with exorbitant, unchecked rates of interest. It is a bad deal, and in most cases, a disgraceful way to soak the poor.

Telephones

Two plans to consider, among the many offered by the major companies, are discounted plans and per-minute plans. If you can hold your long-distance calling to weekends and nighttime (or early morning), the former will be less expensive. If you make many calls during the day, the per-minute plans will be preferable. Once you have considered the type of plan that suits you, you can verify rates by calling the major long-distance companies and allowing them access to an average month's bill. With it, they can simply quote the amount you would have paid under their most applicable plan. The smaller companies, offering savings only on certain types of calls, with use of an access code, are problematic. Some will add hidden charges to your bill or assume all your long-distance billing after you use their code to make just one call.

The Extended Warranty

A customer may run all over town squeezing out the best price on some appliance, machine, or piece of electronic equipment, only to buy an extended-care warranty and hand over a nearly 100 percent profit to the store. Such warranties usually overlap the manufacturer's own warranty. The only time such a warranty is worth considering is for a used car. Then, the premium should not be exorbitant (depending on the condition of the vehicle, it should be about 10 percent of the selling price), and the warranty should be insured in case the company behind it goes out of business.

TELEMARKETERS

No one likes telemarketers. Yet their sales rise by a fifth every year. We are either a lonely race or a spineless one. Many telemarketers represent legitimate operations, but nonetheless, phone sales are a high-pressure tactic. It isn't easy to say no. It literally isn't. Many common phrases of polite rejection can be construed by the telemarketer to mean "Call back," or even "Yes." If you know that you aren't interested, interrupt (think of it as saving the other person's time) and say, "No, and please don't call back." Try to stick to that script. Not that it is poetry, but it should save you further interruption, according to the law. "No, I'm not interested" is totally ineffectual, as it holds forth the hope that you will be at another time.

Whatever the inconvenience of telemarketing, however, it can also disguise crafty criminal activity, and so— remember this— DO NOT EVER GIVE ANY STRANGER OVER THE TELEPHONE ANY NUMBER, NO MATTER HOW THAT PERSON IDEN- TIFIES HIMSELF OR HERSELF. And *any number* means exactly that, because with computer links, a crook with so much as your third-grade homeroom number can hop-to and clean out your bank account.

If all the money given to phony charities went to legiti- mate ones instead, good work in this country could in- crease by 50 percent. People rotten to the core call you up and say that they are collecting for the County Sheriff's Something-or-other, which supports youth basketball and crime prevention. Who wouldn't ante up to the sheriff for the sake of our youth? Meanwhile, precisely 3 percent of what is donated actually goes to the County Sheriff's group. That is a common example. In some cases, legitimate groups hire telemarketing firms at exorbitant commissions like the one mentioned. In other cases, there is no legitimate charity behind a phone solicitation. Don't agree to donate anything over the telephone. If you are remotely interested in the cause, have the telemarketer mail you some information to look over (they probably won't, anyway, unless you agree to make a donation). It must be wrenching for the American Cancer Society or the Salvation Army to see so many millions of well-intentioned dollars going to line the pockets of telemarketers.

SELECTED GLOSSARY

Cash Flow: The ability of income to meet expenditures in a timely way.

Consumer price index (CPI): A measure of inflation or deflation on the household level, as charted by the U.S. Department of Labor. It reflects general household purchases, such as food, clothes, and housing. The resulting change, if any, is known as the cost-of-living index.

Producer Price Index (PPI): The measure of inflation or deflation at the wholesale level, often perceived as a sneak preview of the CPI a year or so down the road.

GET IN TOUCH

Telecommunications Research and Action Center
P.O. Box 12038
Washington, DC 20005
For $3 you receive an updated comparison of residential long-distance rates.

SIX ON THE WEB

www.bbb.org (Better Business Bureau). Has watchdog information on companies and charities.

www.coupon.com (CouponNet). Optimizes the world of "cents-off."

www.eren.doe.gov (Energy Efficiency and Renewable Energy Network–U.S. Department of Energy). Gives advice on reducing home consumption of energy.

www.ftc.gov (Federal Trade Commission Bureau of Consumer Protection). Provides alerts and legislative updates.

www.give.org (National Charities Information Bureau). Rates hundreds of charities.

www.stretcher.com (The Dollar Stretcher). Tips galore, updated weekly, from how to save on everything from gasoline to safe deposit boxes to pudding!

Chapter 7

READY FOR ANYTHING

Financial independence is the overriding goal of long-
term planning. . . . Everyone should have a degree of
independence even while employed, with savings and
protection enough to turn almost any disaster into mere
financial inconvenience. . . . Just as important is retirement planning, a combination of pensions, annuities, savings, and Social Security benefits to provide a comfortable second life after one career is finished. It is
advantageous to cultivate retirement income as early as
possible, as time helps immensely in producing amazingly
large amounts from even a few thousand dollars.

Few folks nowadays can even name the Four Horsemen
of the Apocalypse: Famine, Something, Something, and
Pestilence. People in this country have only rarely wor-
ried about Famine, and as to Something, Something, and
Pestilence, they don't pose a countrywide threat. Threats
to the national well-being seem not to exist. Our country
is stability itself. Over individuals, though, the horsemen
ride hard. Great things happen to individuals; sad or
tragic things happen to individuals, and it is left to individuals to invent their own futures—continuously.

Properly governed, money is crucial to your prevailing through divorce, layoff, relocation, disaster, disability, or just plain disappointment. It provides options. And nothing is cheerier than the warm glow of an option in an otherwise dark time. Given the chance, your money will also provide options over your prosperity. That is the simple premise behind making a serious financial plan.

On the other hand, you can always move in with your brother. You can carry your suitcase in and let someone else go for the trunks, all on the promise to make yourself helpful in the household. (Which you don't really have to do.) That particular long-term plan is not only tried and true but also the basis for many a southern novel. It will always work, unless your brother hears about it far enough in advance. Or unless he was already on his way over to make himself useful in *your* household. As another option, you can raise money to live on by having a big garage sale or perhaps selling pies on the front lawn; in the movies, at least, that always leads to your owning a chain of department stores or a bakery bigger than a Ford plant. People have other peculiar ideas in lieu of long-term planning. Some advance into old age still waiting for an inheritance, despite the fact that no medicine keeps a tightwad alive longer than the aroma of heirs who are waiting.

FORWARD-FACING AGE

Employed or resting (as the English actors used to say when they were out of work), the least important characteristic in financial planning is your age. Some people in their twenties genuinely want to retire by fifty, and they do. Many people in their seventies and eighties are still working, earning more than ever.

Age counts backward to zero, after all. That's the past, which is always fascinating, but it is the future that money can control. Long-term planning is concerned with another age of your life, the forward-facing one, and that is too great an entity to be wrapped up in a couple of digits. Instead of a number, give it dreams and give it fears.

If your long-term planning is based entirely on fears, then you will become nothing but a miser. The more money misers save, the tinier their dreams become until there isn't anything left but old shoes. On the other hand, if your long-term planning is based only on dreams, there will be nothing left but losing lottery tickets—and by the shoeboxful. Along the balance, between the two, lies a life worth living. Can you picture it?

PEEKING INTO OTHER PEOPLE'S THOUGHTS

Person 1.   *Dreams:* To stop working at the age of sixty-two; to personally renovate the old homestead; to live as well in retirement as before, or even better.
Fears: To become a burden to son; to go into debt; to have activities in retirement restricted by tight finances.

Person 2.   *Dreams:* To own enough apartment buildings around town to quit work and become a full-time landlord; never to retire; to be in a position to care for disabled, currently uninsured spouse.
Fears: Medical problem (or death) could leave spouse without a high level of care; reversal in investments.

Person 3. *Dreams:* To build a business in successful restaurant; to buy a bigger house; to buy a lake house; to hand the restaurant over to one of the five children; without specific timetable, to retire with spouse to a place with better weather.
Fears: Care of family in case of personal medical problem; care of business in case of same; none of the children will want the restaurant; leaving enough of an estate so that the restaurant will not have to be sold to settle estate, if one child does someday want it; having enough money for retirement.

Person 4. That's you. Even in the broadest strokes, organize your forward-facing life. A hammock may help.

Before You Lie Down

Brush off all the dead leaves. And then . . .

Many people think that *long-term planning* is *retirement planning.* It isn't. A child saving for a bicycle is involved in long-term planning, of sorts. Yet the fact is that that little kid is doing more about the future than many, many adults making big money right now. People save, of course, in order to buy a home, to send children through college, and also for retirement. Nonetheless, planning has many dimensions where straight savings do not.

When to begin long-term planning: When you are about 22, under otherwise normal circumstances; certainly when you get engaged to be married; and most certainly when you have children.

When most people begin long-term planning: When they are about 32.

When some people begin long-term planning: Well, you can start now, if you want.

Snug but not Smug

If someone has nice banking accounts humming along—a tidy blanket of life insurance, a well-organized portfolio of investments, a trim income tax rate, and logical debt well under control—does that person have a long-term plan? Consider this wise statement: You can't have planning without the planning. Prioritizing and coordination strengthen the power behind assets, making them a whole. In many cases of uncoordinated assets, people are covered in case of unexpected problems or tragedies (fears), but neglect the opportunity to be fully prepared for the good things that they want to make happen (dreams). In your asset ring, then, planning is the very factor that shapes a line of assets into a ring.

Financial planning doesn't have to be complicated or daunting. You are allowed to keep it simple. More important is the fact that people in low-income groups can require sophisticated planning, just as pointedly as can people with buckets of money. As examples of those who might benefit out of proportion to their net worth, consider these: people with many children to send through college; people with serious illnesses; people with a small business, especially partners or sole proprietors. Surprisingly enough, the group needing financial planning more than any other—of whatever level—is made up of people whose assets have to be depleted for one reason or another. Deciding how to shrink an asset ring without damaging its ability to provide and protect is a challenge of immense consequence.

HELP IS ON THE WAY

If you say the words "I guess I could use some advice about financial planning" quietly to yourself, and then get up to check the front window, there is likely to be a line forming on the walk of people more than happy to set up an appointment. Some are outright wizards—if a wizard is a person who can give you a better life than you might have had otherwise. Some don't even know as much as you do, especially if you have read a few scattered paragraphs or every word of this simple book. The SEC will oversee firms with more than $25 million in assets, and states will watch over smaller shops, but there are still ways for an unqualified planner to slip by without official supervision. In any case, most financial planners have unbalanced expertise. They may try to solve your problems largely through the means with which they are most familiar. Or the means by which they make the most money. However, even among qualified and well-intentioned planners, the biggest mistake is in creating a lopsided ring.

Brain Trust. The least expensive way to design and implement a high-quality financial plan is to collect a team of experts, made up of those with whom you normally do business: the stockbroker, insurance agent, accountant, lawyer, banker (or trust officer). Balancing advice and perspective from each, you can develop a general plan for consensus review. The responsibility to update the plan periodically is yours, as is the obligation to speak to a full array of professionals.

On the Staff. In the long-gone days of being filthy rich, one's future was left in the hands of the estate manager, who knew all about Rhodesian railroads and how to make millions in copper without ever getting anywhere near the smudgy stuff. In the fiction of the first half of the twentieth century, the estate manager was handsome, but never enough to steal anyone's affections. Smart but quiet, poor but honest, he always had a pencil-thin mustache—who wouldn't want an estate manager?

Since the power of money has been bestowed on all during the past generation or two, the financial planner has emerged to fill many of the roles of the estate manager. You can't be positive that planners know all about Rhodesian railroads anymore. As a matter of fact, they just aren't at all predictable as a category. To rectify that, a handful of organizations have been started in order to confer some professional ordination on practitioners. The most rigorous and well rounded of all the many designations, however, is *certified financial planner (CFP)*.

Before you see any financial planner, write down on a piece of paper a list of your objectives, your forward-facing life, as it were, reduced to a series of phrases. At the first consultation, a good financial planner will ask about your current situation, discuss your expectations, and try to indicate what is realistic. You will eventually receive a written plan, which starts with the optimizing of your asset ring and projects anticipated changes or developments. If you can, ask another interested professional to peruse the plan. Finally, take out the list of objectives written down before the process even started. Does the plan address each one satisfactorily, or do you truly understand why the priorities shifted? Some of your objectives may have been cockeyed and needed to be corrected by a professional in the business. On the other hand, some financial plans lean into a middle ground of composite expectations, no matter the individual concerns. Use the list to make sure that what started out as your plan ends up as *your* plan.

Checklist to select a financial planner:

1. Know who the planner is. Ask specifically about affiliations with particular companies and products. All financial planners must file a disclosure, called Form ADV, listing qualifications, fees, and violations (if any); ask for a complete copy of it.

2. Financial planners may take a fee, earn a commission on products sold to you, or charge a combination of the two. There is nothing necessarily wrong with any of the methods, though a fee-only charge results in the fewest complaints. Because the bases of remuneration can vary so widely, understand them thoroughly. If the planner is not direct and forthcoming about all the ways that your account can generate fees and commissions, move without delay to one who is.

3. Make sure the planner knows in advance of your first appointment about any standing relationships you have with brokers or agents; some planners will not take an account unless they manage it themselves or through their own associates.

4. Some planners make a specialty of working with people in a certain profession or situation.

5. You will normally engage a financial planner for a long, open-ended time frame, not for a single fix-up.

MARTHA AND NAN SPEAK FRANKLY ABOUT RETIREMENT

"I'll do your financial planning," Nan said to Martha one morning, when Martha was outside reading a book about Chile. "First of all, how much do you expect to receive in Social Security?"

"That's where I'm going," Martha said, holding up the book.

"Oh, yours is the same as mine, just about. Earning $52,000, age thirty-five, we'll get about $14,000 per annum. OK. How much do you have in savings? About $10,540, as I happen to recall. That will be worth, at 8 percent, about $63,240 in thirty years," said Nan. "What about IRA accounts?"

"I spent the $10,000 already. I'm going on a cruise around South America this fall."

"No savings. No IRA accounts. No investment portfolio. What on earth . . ."

"I can always live in Chile for $14,000. Fish and grapes . . . some little village."

"Look at me, I'll get my Social Security, of course. I bought an annuity with my inheritance, so at retirement age I'll get a minimum of $16,000 per year from that. Moreover, I've been putting $1,000 away every year since I was twenty. That will be up to almost 300,000 bucks when I'm sixty-five. Say I'll get taxed out of one-third of it. That's $200,000, and at 6 percent, I'll take home $12,000 a year. Even after only ten years working at the factory-that-doesn't-make-anything, I'm already vested for a pension of $8,000 per year. So, if I quit right now, having contributed a grand total of only $25,000 of my own money, do you know how much I would earn per year in my retirement?"

"You haven't been to Greece. I have."

"Fifty thousand per year, and in perpetuity. And I'm only thirty-five. And I've barely even begun to start investing."

Martha stood up. "Are you done making my financial plan?"

> "You're going to be poor, you know."
>
> "And you," Martha said as grandly as she could on her way out, "will be Chile-less."
>
> "Fifty thousand," Nan screamed after her with a maniacal laugh. "Fifty thousand dollars, Americano."

NEW YEARS

For the first time in your life, because of retirement planning, you will be in a position to decide how much you should get paid. Through a variety of means, you can make the provisions for the level of income you want or need. You can even give yourself a raise over the amount you took home for working forty hours per week.

At lower and middle incomes, a usual target is to reap a little more than three-quarters of your peak job earnings. That is the amount earned over an average of the best (usually the final) years of a career. A woman who earned $100,000 per year at her final job level will probably live very comfortably in retirement on $75,000 per year. Actually, the decrease by a quarter would not necessarily affect your standard of living since a number of job-related expenses, including some regarding clothes and transportation, will disappear when you stop working. (Keeping a job can be an expensive proposition.) In addition, contributions to savings, including some life insurance policies, will diminish. Many people nowadays are actually trying to provide for 100 percent of their high-average annual earnings, in view of the common perception that Social Security will be extinct or curtailed in the coming decades. Keep in mind, though, that your forward-facing plans for retirement make a big difference in how much you will need. If you are looking forward to moving to a smaller home or a less-expensive region of the country, you may, of course, adjust your needs downward. If you plan to spend all day everyday at the racetrack, you may adjust your needs upward.

Depending on your age, you also have to consider that inflation will work on the value of money over the years. In spending power, $50,000 today is likely to match $120,000 in thirty years. Even a mildly aggressive stock portfolio should stay ahead of inflation, but don't be fooled into thinking that once you have accumulated what looks like a fortune, you can let up on saving. You won't know for certain how rich you are until you get home from the grocery store on your first day of retirement.

A financial planner can help to calculate your precise requirements. However, in lieu of formulas, use your gray matter for a few minutes to ponder the following:

• **If you are in your twenties,** it doesn't matter how much you will need in retirement; just start socking some money away. Obviously a jet ski is more fun than a retirement account, but a dollar saved at the age of twenty-five will be the same amount at sixty-five as $4.50 saved at forty-five (at 8 percent annual interest). Save now, jet ski later.

• **If you are in your thirties,** you probably know what you do for a living, at long last; it may have been touch and go when you were in your twenties. Project how much you can earn in your chosen field by the time you are a big shot at sixty. Expect to have a good career and start planning ways to provide for a comfortable retirement based generally on that figure. However, if you are self-employed, expect to have a terrible, disappointing, and miserable career. That is, don't delude yourself that money is veritably *bound* to start flooding in by the time you're fifty. Just in case there's a riptide by the time you're sixty, establish a serious retirement plan.

Basic checklist:

1. Initiate an IRA or similar tax-advantaged savings, putting away even as little as a couple of hundred dollars a year.

2. If you favor whole life insurance, starting a policy when you are younger will help you to contract a low premium for the life of the policy.

• **If you are in your forties and fifties,** with a fairly good idea of what you will need in retirement, you should also have a good idea of what sort of company benefits you will be able to count on, if any. You should be able to calculate most of your sources of retirement income and add to them, if necessary.

• **If you are in your sixties or beyond,** and still haven't thought hard about retirement, you are far from alone in the matter. Quite a few people just keep charging ahead without pausing to ponder their dotage. Other people find themselves suddenly widowed or divorced, and have to learn how retirement works, all at once and all by themselves. Don't worry, there are always options. (The rumor that there aren't is mainly meant to scare people still in their twenties.)

Later checklist:

1. Investigate all company pension plans and fully funded tax-advantaged savings plans, such as 401(k) plans.

2. Balance these savings with cash assets and a stock portfolio.

3. Verify the status of your Social Security account.

4. Establish the income target needed for a comfortable retirement, perhaps with the guidance of a financial planner.

5. Have a valid will. If your estate may be worth more than $600,000, work with an estate lawyer to begin planning ways to reduce the tax burden.

SOCIAL SECURITY

> We can never insure one hundred percent of the population against one hundred percent of the hazards and vicissitudes of life, but we have tried to frame a law which will give some measure of protection to the average citizen and to his family against the loss of a job and against poverty-ridden old age.
> —*Franklin Delano Roosevelt,*
> *on signing the Social Security Act, August 14, 1935*

Social Security is some measure of protection; it is not a jackpot. Of course, the talk these days is that it will fold long before any of us see any of the benefits. It will survive, because it is essential to the national economy. But the threat of it collapsing has certainly acted as an electric cattle prod on a whole generation of Americans. Zzzzzzzzz. Your future is in your own hands. Zzzzzzzzz.

Figure on Social Security benefits only as a backup for your own pension and savings. Zzzzzzzzz. That's what Roosevelt wanted you to do all along, anyway, you know.

Generally, those covered have worked (and paid social security taxes) during at least forty quarters during their lives, or have earned more money during a lesser number of quarters. The computation of the retirement benefit tries to reward people who contribute more over the years in Social Security taxes, but it is also weighted to the good of people at lower income levels. Currently, the spread is about $600 to $1,900 per month. Since Social Security benefits are indexed to the inflation rate, you can figure on payouts with earning power in that range, whenever you do retire. The presence of dependents, including spouses (and qualifying divorced spouses), minor children, and disabled adult children can increase the amount. A person who has earned Social Security benefits in his or her own right can't also collect benefits from a spouse's account.

Tip: when to pull the string—Retirement benefits generally begin when the socially secured person reaches 65 to 67 years. However, a lesser benefit can begin with age 62. And a bolstered benefit comes with later retirement from 67 to 70 years. It's a bit of a crapshoot, all other things being equal: Nab more money in the short run by retiring early or go for the bigger payments later on?

Tip: just ask—The Social Security Administration will inform you now of the exact amount that you can expect to receive (even though subsequent factors may eventually impact the payment). The form required (SSA-7004-PC) is available at your local post office, or from any Social Security office.

Tip: the family — Even if a Social Security recipient dies, the widowed spouse, minor children, or disabled adult children can continue to receive payments.

COMPANY IS HERE

Company benefits range from plans that are more hoax than help to cushioned litters on which some corporations send their beloved workers off into the world of retirement. Many company pensions promise a monthly payout of a *fixed amount,* based on the worker's income level and years of service. In times of inflation, though, a fixed amount droops in buying power after only a few years. A fixed-income pension has to be bolstered by other savings income, or partially reinvested in order to constantly correct for inflation. Although company plans naturally vary, the flattest advice is that whenever a company will match contributions to a savings plan, sign up and go without bread if necessary to stay with it. That's free money, make no mistake. One of the worst temptations regarding company plans that contain a choice (which many now do) is the tendency to listen to office scuttlebutt regarding the best options. If you ask around, you may be astonished at how many people made certain retirement decisions, just because that's what Joey did. Who's Joey?

The *401(k) plan* came by its quaint name because it is section 401 of the Internal Revenue Code. Clause (k) therein allows people to effectively defer paying income tax on earnings diverted directly into an account maintained by the employer. And it is in 401(k) plans that employers often match contributions, in varying proportions, over and above the employee's regular salary. Perhaps the most notable aspect of a 401(k) plan, though, is that it is fully portable. An employee who jumps around from job to job may never accrue pension benefits from any one company but may haul the 401(k) money around in an ever bigger, albeit battered, case.

OTHER TEMPTING OFFERS

The *Individual Retirement Account (IRA),* a special type of nest egg from the IRS point of view, has one stinging drawback: You can't touch your own money. You can look at it from afar, but it's behind unbreakable glass, and you can't touch it until you are fifty-nine. Created in 1982, the IRA is an enticing proposition in that both the principal deposited and the interest accrued are tax deferred. Many people believe that the main benefit of an IRA is that they will pay all income taxes on it when they retire, when, so the wisdom goes, their tax rate will be lower. Think about it, though. Earners' income tax rate isn't apt to be much lower when they retire than when they were in their twenties and just starting out. It may not even be much lower in retirement than it was right before retirement, especially for people blessedly awash in retirement income.

Actually, the true benefit of the IRA lies in having use of the government's money for so many years and years. Instead of tax deferred, it should be called an interest-free loan, because that is the potent aspect of it. If someone else will give you an interest-free loan, in exchange for taxing a quarter or a third of the gain off the interest that has accumulated in forty years, grab it quickly.

But wait! Do you want the interest-free loan in exchange for a tax bite at the end, or would you rather buy what is behind the curtain marked Roth-IRA. That is a new variation on the IRA theme, by which you pay your income tax now—honest citizen that you are—deposit the remainder in the account, and earn tax-free interest for forty years. What to do, what to do. "Tax-free" is the absolute greatest two-word phrase in the language, the bee's knees, and the only thing that many a wastrel ever had to learn about investing. Take the Roth-IRA . . . no, the traditional . . . no, the . . .

Each can be preferable in certain circumstances. As long as the account remains intact for five years, the Roth-IRA allows depositors to remove the whole amount for college tuition or to put it toward a first home, as well as for retirement. On the other hand, if you are fairly certain that you will have a significantly lower tax rate when you retire, consider the traditional, tax-deferred IRA. On the other hand, some people, understandably, like the idea of getting the tax payment over with so that they know everything in the account is theirs, theirs, theirs. On the other hand, the fact is that the IRA became much more intriguing with the choice of the Roth-type account.

Another type of tax-benefit account is the *Keogh account*, which is akin to the traditional IRA, but for self-employed people. Deposits into an IRA are capped at a few thousand dollars per year, depending on particular circumstances, but Keogh accounts have a much higher cap, of about $30,000 per year.

The *annuity* is the old-fashioned way to provide for retirement. With all the other fashions and inventions that might clutter a retirement plan, the annuity is still the big comfy armchair that has a place in any room. At the end, the annuity pays a monthly stipend for as long as the benefactor lives. A comforting thought! The front-end payment is usually a lump sum, and so the earlier it is purchased, the more money it will pay out. Many people who receive a windfall or inheritance when they are young purchase an annuity. Some people at retirement age transfer a lump sum from a whole life insurance policy into an annuity, guaranteeing monthly payments that will be eternal, as far as the policyholder is concerned. In the old days, Papa and Mama would buy an annuity for their slightly dizzy son or daughter, handing over a wad of cash up front for the guarantee that the little dope would at least have something to live on in retirement.

Typically purchased from insurance companies, brokerages, and trust companies, annuities pay different rates of interest, but are often quite competitive. Under the terms of most, money cannot be withdrawn for any reason whatsoever. Income tax on the accumulating interest defers until payment begins at retirement age. Annuities can be customized, especially as to whether the payment is preset or dependent on the growth rate of investments behind the annuity.

ONE SECOND OF RETIREMENT

The word "retired" is something like the word "age." Both look backward, not forward. A person does indeed retire from some past activity, such as working at an office. But what of it? Who wants to define life by what he or she used to do?

Retirement describes the first instant. As to the years of life and challenge that are ahead—other jobs or good hard volunteer work, learning something new or perfecting something second nature, seeing the world with new eyes—that deserves a fitting word, such as Liberty. Anything is possible, but to end where this chapter began, keep your eye on your long-term planning.

Liberty is not free.

SELECTED GLOSSARY

Employee stock ownership plan (ESOP): Part of many employee pension plans that gives employees shares purchased for them by the company through a large loan. The company gets the cash and employees get the shares. On a large scale, the ESOP can be used in an employee buyout of a company.

Lump sum distribution: A pension or life insurance benefit taken in the form of a single payment. If there is a choice, the decision may have tax or planning implications over installment payments.

Real Estate Investment Trust (REIT): A fund in which the underlying investments are properties, some of which may enjoy tax advantages. A REIT is akin to a mutual fund.

GET IN TOUCH

American Institute of Certified Public Accountants
Harborside Financial Center
201 Plaza 3
Jersey City, NJ 07311–3881
201–938–3000; 888–999–9256; **www.cpapfs.org**
Professional association of CPAs.

Employee Benefit Research Institute
2121 K St., Suite 600
Washington, DC 20037
202–659–0670
Sends comprehensive or specific material regarding pensions and other benefits.

Institute of Certified Financial Planners
7600 E. Eastman Ave., Suite 301
Denver, CO 80231
800–282–7526
Offers brochures on planning and can help you to find a CFP in your locality.

National Center for Financial Education
2512 Horton St.
San Diego, CA 92101
619–232–8811
For brochures on all aspects of money management and on using a financial planner.

Older Women's League
666 11th St., NW, Suite 700
Washington, DC 20001
202–783–6686
Advocate group that distributes brochures and books.

Pension Rights Center
918 16th St., NW, Suite 704
Washington, DC 20006
202–296–3776
Can field questions and also send brochures.

Social Security Administration
6401 Security Blvd.
Baltimore, MD 21235
800–772–1213
The Social Security Administration's Public Information
Distribution Center offers dozens of free brochures (P.O.
Box 17743, Baltimore, MD 21235).

SIX ON THE WEB

www.financenter.com (FinanCenter). Provides step-by-
step formulas for calculating retirement income, car payments, and many other planning aids.

www.ssa.gov (Social Security On Line). Gives information on programs, including your own account information and projected benefits.

www.reverse.org (National Center for Home Equity
Conversion). A no-nonsense site that will explain the
proper uses, as well as the unfortunate abuses, of the
reverse mortgage for older homeowners. Includes a calcu-
lator to ascertain the payments that a reverse mortgage
would generate under specific circumstances.

www.aoa.dhhs.gov/retirement/fpfr.html (Administration on Aging). Provides dozens of links to other websites
directed at retirement planning.

www.estateplanning.com (Schumacher Publishing).
Emphasizes tools by which to estimate estate taxes, and

offers referral service for locating an attorney specializing in estate planning.

www.hancock.com (John Hancock). Customized tools help put such goals as long-term care, college tuition, and retirement savings in perspective for individuals.

Chapter 8
NEW STARTS

Changes come over the course of anyone's life, and money will be some part of each one. . . . Marriage, or any serious relationship between two people, has to include an understanding of money and what it really means to them. Consulting an accountant or planner in advance is a way to see the impact of joint financial decisions before taking them. . . . Divorce is often negotiated on many levels, but the financial ones must count invisible assets as well as tangible ones. Keeping copies of all financial records, as early as possible, helps to expedite an advantageous settlement. . . . Anyone with any assets whatsoever should keep an inventory of them, in case of emergency or death, because tracking down far-flung assets can be hopeless otherwise. As a legal representation of a person's wishes, a will does not have to be complicated or expensive to be highly effective.

An actor who had signed a contract to write his memoirs was faced with a terrible problem. He couldn't remember very much—when it came right down to blank pads and sharp pencils—about his life. He looked at scrapbooks and old letters, but it was no use. Then he came across his financial ledgers and the memories came jumping off the pages, neatly dated and in order.

Money doesn't define a life, but it is there at every hint of change. Like water, it can be beneficial or destructive, especially in the way it can find tiny cracks in a relationship, such as marriage, and slowly but surely make gaping holes out of them. People can get into a lot of trouble looking only at the water and never at the boat.

It does not say much for human nature that something as delightful as money can be so destructive, but that is the difference between money and water. Water is something; money is nothing, except what people believe it is. The fact that you have some money gives other people the right to believe whatever they want about you. Some will always think you are rich, no matter what—and let you buy lunch. Some will always think you are poor. You can give the same exact present to five people. Two will think you are generous beyond reckoning, two will think you are tighter than bark on a tree, and one will reserve judgment until the thing has been returned to the store to see how much it cost.

What other people want to believe about you and your money is far beyond your control. Unfortunately, so is what *you* believe about you and your money, in a lot of cases. Self-worth as expressed in dollars is often tightly woven with self-worth as in enthusiasm for life. That's sad. It's not surprising then that this past century worshipped the rich. But it's sad when people let money matter too much.

Money is at its best when it doesn't matter at all. The first seven chapters of this book discussed ways to acquire and use money. Perhaps there should have been one more chapter, on the subject of having a ball with a pocketful of money. The need for advice on that particular subject is surprisingly low, however.

The goal of personal finance is not to have the most money; that's a sporting proposition. This is all about your life, feeling comfortable, and growing rich, however much money there is.

MARRIAGE

A marriage is one of the most complicated financial mergers possible. If two businesses decided to blend assets and start spending each other's money, there would be a stack of contracts up to the moon. And before there were contracts there would be teams of chattering lawyers making sure that both companies understood every nuance of the merger. Not a bad idea. To make sure that both people in a marriage start out with the same understanding, it would be advantageous for a couple to have a relatively arduous discussion about their money, perhaps with an accountant or planner who can describe the ramifications of various decisions. Niggling misunderstandings about money almost invariably grow, scooping up other problems as they do, until a quarrel that could once have been about a simple matter turns out later to include just about *everything*. If there are problems, the simplest, and yet hardest, way to get past them is to look each other in the eye and recall that money doesn't really matter. When that belief can be made to last for at least three seconds, without someone bursting out with "Sure, that's easy for you to say. You don't even . . ." it can make for a starting point.

Some couples combine all their assets and accounts. Constant communication is necessary, if only to keep either from inadvertently bouncing a check. Still, the combination often works best when one person or the other takes a fuller interest in the bookkeeping. Other couples maintain quite separate accounts and split household bills down the middle, or according to some other formula. Either method can work. Just walking down the street on a Saturday morning, we can hear couples discussing their finances—at about eighteen decibels.

Yellow house: They are fighting because one person fritters away money, while the other scrimps and saves a nickel at a time. (Apparently, they keep combined accounts.) They could shop together to try to come to an accord as to how they spend their money. They could try to implement a budget, though that would only seem to punish the freewheeler; it could be that the tightwad is the one going too far. As a pressure valve, each of them could open a small, private account to allow for a discretionary allowance.

Brown house: One of them—the one doing most of the hollering—is going to have to take a part-time job in order to meet half the household expenses. Meanwhile, the other has no such problems, having just received a raise. (They have separate accounts.) Someone is being stubborn. And it may well be the person who is strapped, in the misguided name of independence. If it is the other one, old moneybags, it would be quite reprehensible. Mutual support is the essence of marriage. Anyway, there really ought to be a national holiday when all stubbornness is outlawed, just to see what would be left—considerably fewer fights over money, for one thing.

However the money is managed, if steep expenses are straining the budget and causing tension, consider moving into a smaller home, surviving with one car, or yanking out the television and most of the telephone equipment.

Children: Children are wonderful creations (most of them, anyway), but in purely economic terms, one child equals one Rolls Royce—and that's without even college tuition. To raise a child through high school graduation costs between $100,000 and $200,000, depending on what sneakers he or she wears in middle school. Actually, parents should pause to consider that the difference between a humble upbringing and a lavish one is $100,000. Some part of the reason is that parents no longer make decisions for their children, as they once did. Restaurant chains, entertainment companies, sports franchises, clothing companies, and other potent marketing organizations reach children more and more effectively than parents do.

It may seem as if children decide what is important—but they really don't decide at all. Disney does. Nike does. McDonald's does. Pepsi does. When cigarette and beer companies are seen to plant decisions in the minds of children, there is an outcry. Yet an even greater corporate commune is raising many kids, and so parents should keep in mind that allowing children to make decisions over spending is tantamount to letting strangers tap into that $100,000 of your money. You might give your children fifty cents (that is, a weekly allowance of about fifty cents for each year in their age) as a fair lesson in money management.

The best estimate for college costs is that tuition with room and board will go up a minimum of 6 percent per year. Part of that increase is a private spiral of inflation; the higher the costs, the more scholarship aid schools have to offer, and so the higher the cost they must charge those who can afford it. A child who is 6 today will probably face costs of about $60,000 per year at a private four-year college (costing $30,000 today). The government is finally trying to assist parents, by offering tax-free interest income on both U.S. savings bonds and the Roth-IRA, when the funds are used directly for tuition. So, the time to start saving for a child's education is when he or she is still a gleam in your eye, because time is very much on the saver's side. Several of the major brokerages have special accounts with reduced commissions and planning services just for college savings. Also, some schools offer tempting prepayment plans, by which a reasonable charge for a four-year education is locked in, after the parents make a partial or full payment ten or more years in advance. Refunds are available if the child ends up not attending college after all.

Parents who still see no way to cover costs sometimes make a whole career move for the sake of the children, since college employees often receive free or discounted tuition for their children. All other things being equal, it could turn into quite a bonus.

Some car buyers, some airline passengers, and, alas, some students pay more than others for the exact same thing. In determining need, colleges typically presume that parents can contribute a sum equal to 10 to 12 percent of their assets to the cost of a four-year education, although other expenses, including other college-age children, mitigate even that formula. Some parents go to great lengths to hide assets from schools or to shift them advantageously between themselves and their children. Hiding assets is rather smarmy. Instead, groom your child into the kind of prospect the colleges want. For most entering students, financial aid can be a negotiating point, one way a college puts itself on sale for students it wants badly enough.

SEPARATION AND DIVORCE

Amazingly and astonishingly, some divorces proceed without a hitch, smooth as silk. Two people make a decision, the resulting choices seem obvious to both, and—happily ever after—they even laugh on the phone together a couple of times per year. And some people fall out of an airplane, hop up off the ground, and are glad to have finally worked out the crick in their necks. Divorce is so often a wrenching ordeal that it seems as if it is supposed to be that way. On every level in an unhappy divorce, money begins to matter totally out of proportion, as the last form of communication left.

Obviously, it helps to plan far in advance for a divorce, starting with a prenuptial agreement listing the important assets of the marriage and to whom they will revert, should there be a division. But that strikes most people as a self-fulfilling prophecy. If the thought of seeing a divorce lawyer seems a bit premature on the eve of a wedding, a couple might consider asking an accountant to draw up an inventory of important assets, as a mutual acknowledgment of whence they came. Without such documentation or a prenuptial agreement, it will not matter in most cases in whose name assets happen to be at the time of a divorce; they will be presumed to belong to the marriage. Unfortunately, the assets in joint accounts sometimes don't make it to the divorce proceedings, if one person or the other takes advantage by absconding with all the cash. It seems futile to suggest that people establish separate accounts should divorce become a possibility; by the time the suggestion is made, a disreputable spouse will have already hollowed out the till. At the same time, some people run up outrageous credit card debt on joint accounts.

If there is a serious stir of trouble in the marriage, rev up the photocopier and duplicate the following: all pertinent account agreements; savings passbooks and other banking statements; insurance policies; benefits statements; deeds; contracts for mortgages, leases, loans, and anything else for which the couple signed; promissory notes and agreements regarding money loaned out to others; documents from previous divorces (if any); wills; major receipts; bonds or stock certificates.

The foregoing list should give you an idea of the big pile of assets that will be turned, come a divorce, into two smaller piles of assets. Insurance policies, pensions, and Social Security benefits should be on the table, as should real property, of course. Other, offbeat assets that become part of the bargaining process are memberships at private clubs, parking or beach permits, certain premiums earned through telephone or credit card companies, tax exemptions for dependent children, and, most important of all, professional degrees. Many courts recognize the earning power of an advanced degree received during marriage as a particularly important financial asset. Money that is owed is also on the table, to be settled in the divorce.

The court's job is to weigh all the assets of the marriage and divide them equitably. Community property states try not to complicate the court agenda by making it construct a history of the marriage. In those states, the court tries to do no more than draw a line down the middle of everything accumulated or developed during the course of the marriage. Other states allow extenuating circumstances to be taken into account. The only therapeutic aspect to the process at its worst becomes evident at the time of the divorce: One may well hate the old spouse more than anyone else on earth—and then one gets to know the divorce lawyer.

Some divorce lawyers cannot be trusted to hold the train tickets, let alone to give birth to the rest of your life. Some, on the other hand, are too good at what they do. And what many clients tell them to do, vaguely, is: "Whatever happens, don't let that so-and-so get away with anything. I don't care who gets the money, as long as it isn't that idiot I married." And so it won't be, because divorces that spiral into vindication cost a lot of money in legal fees. To contain the cost of divorce, in the short or long run, interview three or four recommended lawyers and choose one who is thorough and organized, and one who will explain ways to simplify and expedite the proceeding. An overly aggressive lawyer may only exacerbate your situation. Perhaps you genuinely want a contentious, ruinous, and protracted divorce; some people undoubtedly have reasons for exactly that. Others, however, are drawn into a Hundred Years' War without seeming to know how it happened. If the divorce terms are fairly simple and completely amicable, a family lawyer can draft the papers that will eventually make it final for both parties. Another lawyer should nonetheless look it over, just to make sure it is fair to both people. If the divorce is not quite so amicable, but not overly complicated, a paid mediator can sometimes oversee a settlement in lieu of formal (and expensive) court proceedings.

When it is a family that is divorcing, as opposed to merely a couple, child custody is the major consideration, overall and in financial terms. The most disgraceful fallout from divorce is the failure of some parents to pay the mandated child support. Perhaps someday, financial institutions will arrange bonds for child support, by which they would effectively transfer the payment from one spouse to the other, and guarantee it in any case. A third party might dilute the resentment that keeps some people from complying and would also be in a better position than a single parent to collect late payments.

JUST IN CASE . . .

With all due respect and sorrow and all that, should you "go south" unexpectedly, the relatives have to become the top priority. They might be distracted from their grief by the challenge of patching together your financial empire. Or they might be saddened by the necessity. In the days when people lived in hollows and gulches, it couldn't have been as big a problem. Each gulch had an average of one bank, and so everybody knew where everybody else's account could be found. For all anyone knows nowadays, you could have a little money stashed away in every time zone between here and Calcutta. There are two precautions that can make the whole process much easier on survivors.

The first precaution is to make an inventory of, basically, your life. (Allow about a half hour):

Step 1: Get a couple of cookies and put them on the kitchen counter.

Step 2: Bring back a pencil and a piece of paper. Are you back?

Step 3: List all of the following:

- Banks (names of all institutions, types of accounts, account numbers, location of bankbooks).
- Life insurance policies (name of company, type of policy, policy number, location of policy).
- Other insurance policies (company, type, and policy number; location of policies).
- Deeds (with location) and real property (including valuables that may not be obvious, such as jewelry).
- Bonds, stock certificates, and cash (description and location).
- Debts (including terms, with location of loan agreement and stubs or receipts).
- Safe deposit box (noting where the box is located and where your key is kept).
- Brokerage (name of broker, account number).
- Professionals (any lawyer, accountant, or banker familiar with your finances).

Step 4: When you are finished, you can have the cookies.

Note: You should not indicate where you want such assets to go. This isn't a will; it's an inventory.

You would be aghast at how much of a hard-earned fortune can recede silently to the state because relatives simply do not know where to find it. And you would be dumbstruck at how much cash and jewelry goes to the dump, hidden away in coats, drawers, and mayonnaise jars. With a treasure map, in the form of your inventory, the relatives can find every last ruby. However, there is one last problem. Now that you have the inventory of your assets, you have to hide *it*. The safe deposit box is the most obvious place, though gaining access to a box sometimes takes time, should you be incapacitated. Put another copy of the inventory in a sturdy envelope marked, "In the Event of My Death" with your initials, and give it to a close relative to keep in a different safe deposit box, or leave a copy in your lawyer's safe.

The second precaution in order to save your survivors unnecessary torment is the Last Will and Testament. It will outline your specific directions in dispersing the estate, although most states have guidelines nonetheless. Most notably, be aware that you can't cut your spouse out of your will.

The will can be handwritten and duly witnessed in some states. Fill-in-the-blank forms are available, though hard to recommend except in rudimentary cases. Without any will, the state will distribute an estate's assets according to a standard formula. That process can consume considerable time, since the identity of all survivors must be legally established before any settlement.

For a minimum of about $200, an estate lawyer will draw up a valid will to expedite the distribution and to carry out specific bequests. If your estate is worth more than $600,000, the lawyer can also work through plans to avoid inordinate estate taxes.

BANKRUPTCY

Just as some people are good at miniature golf and others are good at watercolor, some are good at bankruptcy. They hop from bad credit to terrible credit to no credit without slipping a whit from a mighty fine standard of living. Such people make any nice, dull, bill-paying person long for the days of debtors' prisons, stockades, and mushy tomatoes, on the plate or in the face, for people who go bankrupt.

As it is, however, most people are not good at bankruptcy. They cannot pay their bills due to unfair events (or perfectly fair events and miserable planning), and as a first step, their creditors turn any overdue accounts over to collection agencies. The collector takes a hefty cut, if and when the bill is paid, and so the mere act of forcing a creditor to take such a step is bound to damage a person's credit report. Before it reaches that stage, however, there is still hope, in many cases. When a bill becomes two payment periods late, a person may begin to wish it away. That has not been found to work in any cases recorded so far. However, a customer who contacts creditors directly may be able to establish an advantageous payment schedule, especially if there have been extenuating circumstances. If the creditors are unyielding, the customer should still refrain from lying down in despair; there will be time for that later. Nonprofit credit-counseling services can intercede with creditors, after the customer has

begun a program of supervised reorganization. To reiterate, quite a few people neglect the window of opportunity
to help themselves out of trouble.

Some debts are monumental, particularly in cases of
small-business failure or uncovered medical costs. Sometimes, in the face of layoff, the ability to repay even me-
dium-size debts is curtailed. By that time, life is no fun.
Collectors call as often and as aggressively as the law
allows. It is rather depressing that federal law has to for-
bid them from swearing. Or from making physical
threats.

Bankruptcy protection is a serious step, but the time
has probably arrived whenever mortgage default is a possibility, when eviction looms and your family has nowhere
to go, or when other debt-related problems curtail your
ability to earn money.

Before declaring bankruptcy (through a court filing),
speak to a credit counselor, or a lawyer if possible. Sometimes bank officers will help with advice. Sometimes they
won't let you in the lobby, it's true, but not if the cause of
the problem was misfortune and not flagrant irresponsi-
bility. The reason to ask for advice is that the types of
bankruptcy vary in severity and in subsequent impact. In
any case, it takes ten years to return to the land of the
living as far as credit is concerned. Some companies and
lawyers try to take advantage of people undergoing bankruptcy. Don't let anyone delude you about the fact that
bankruptcy is a slow and careful process, without any
room for the quick fix or shortcut.

THE BOSS WORKS OVERTIME

Look carefully at the faces on a crowded subway or at the beach. Those are not mere human beings reading their newspapers or dripping suntan oil all over the towel. Those are entrepreneurs, all of them. America is a nation of people getting ready to start their own businesses. A swell little magazine, a fishing shop, or jet-fighter production—everyone nurtures an idea. A single meal can lead to a surge in business activity. The cook goes to bed insulted if no one at the table suggests that she must absolutely start her own restaurant. *If it was such a good meal, why didn't anyone say that I should start a restaurant?* she thinks darkly, and then decides to open one anyway.

I'll show them, she says to herself, thus offering the most popular reason to start a new business. By the next morning, she has decided to forget the restaurant and bottle the meal for the grocery store—Allie's Mediterranean Chicken in bottles. While sitting on the patio before lunch, designing the label for the bottle, she looks up and goes out of business. It would mean cooking the same meal for the rest of her life, and sliding it into bottles. She decides to write a cookbook with the recipe and go into publishing instead. Over lunch, she goes out of business again. "This is the worst chicken in history," she says, staring down at her leftovers from dinner.

New businesses can be divided into two categories: large enterprises demanding a serious amount of start-up capital, and tiny monogram ones that emerge without any fanfare, solely on the talent of the proprietor. When it comes to the monogram type of small business, it is likely to operate out of the home. In fact, cottage industry is back, a century after most tweed weavers and cigar rollers left their front rooms for regular jobs. Today's cottage industries have been made possible by personalized technology and the overall dependence of business on a flexible workforce. Many of the new troops report that they are much more productive working alone at home than they were amid the distractions and interruptions of the typical office.

One way to start in business at home is to establish freelance or consulting accounts even before leaving other employment. It's a good idea to make a trial run of some sort, because the emotional toll of facing crises and even triumphs all alone can seem unacceptably hard.

Home Business Checklist:

1. Separate work and home as much as possible by designating a room or corner solely for the business, and also by keeping regular hours. Learn to leave your home behind, even though you are at home, and likewise to leave work, even though it beckons from the other room.

2. Maintain separate accounts and books. For both tax and planning reasons, you must be able to see the business finances clearly, unfettered by domestic expenses.

3. Be stringent with friends and relatives. None of them will believe in their hearts that you work at all if you work at home, and so it is up to you to maintain strict and consistent policies about playing hooky or otherwise taking time off.

Whether the business is as large as a new manufacturing facility or as small as a freelance operation, the goal even before starting either type is to reduce the risk, shaving a mountain into a molehill.

Shave the Risk:

1. Learn much more about the business than you think you have to. Go to school on someone else's time by taking a job in the industry. If you are thinking of stealing Allie's idea for bottled chicken, get at least a part-time job in a grocery store and learn how it works.

2. Obviously, a course at a school or small-business incubation center has to help, but even more important are the seminars given by state- and federal-tax agencies. Understand business taxes well in advance of opening a business.

3. Whether you borrow money to start the business or spend your own, have enough on hand to weather one bad year (two in the restaurant business and perhaps more in other industries). Optimists succeed. Pessimists survive. Be both, if you want to do both.

4. Everyone who has a business is in sales. Get out of the office, especially if it is a home office, and become known to people. Many people starting a business spend inordinate money on swank offices or accoutrements intended to create an image. Don't hide behind all that folderol. *You* are the image that counts.

Another way to shave the risk is to purchase an existing business, though the premium added to the price for a going enterprise makes the financing a steeper climb and adds an element of danger from another direction. A business based on the personal popularity of the previous owner is always tempting, since the balance sheets will be plump, but beware that there is no one more disloyal than a customer loyal to somebody else.

The large small business, with real estate commitments, employees, and a credit line, is braced by business procedure, including a detailed business plan. The monogram business, operated out of a home and financed through savings, probably won't have a business plan. It should, though, because efficiency is even more important to a one-person operation than to a bigger shop. Write a memo to yourself covering the points listed in a business plan (a short description of the business; longer ones of the product; initial and projected marketing, financial, management, and production plans).

The simplest form of business is the sole proprietorship established by filing a "Doing Business As" form or DBA, with the country or state. It will allow you to open a checking account and perhaps to file with the state for the collection of taxes. It will also allow customers or others who say they were harmed by your business to sue you for your personal assets. Insurance companies will cover many types of businesses for liability. Incorporation will protect personal assets, although the business ones will still be at risk in the event of a suit. The various types of business organization also have tax implications, and so it is not necessarily a case of working your way up to incorporation or outgrowing a sole proprietorship.

SELECTED GLOSSARY

Executor: The person designated to oversee an estate.

Intestate: Having no valid will. A deceased person who left an estate without a will is said to have died intestate.

Living trust: A means of smoothing the transition of a person's estate, so that he or she can control it quite effectively while alive and then direct its use even after probate. Fundamentally, it organizes the estate and allows all heirs to understand its eventual dispersal while the person is still alive. The living trust can also have tax implications for those with an estate worth more than $600,000.

Living will: A legal document expressing a person's wishes regarding his or her own care in the event of total incapacitation. It usually indicates the circumstances under which the person would just as soon be allowed to die without further treatment.

Probate: The legal process by which an estate is assessed, heirs verified, and assets distributed.

S Corporation: A type of organization that enjoys some of the legal structure of a corporation, but with simpler tax treatment.

KEEP IN TOUCH

American Financial Services Association
919 18th St., NW
Washington, DC 20006
202–296–5544
Offers consumer information, including a brochure, "What You Should Know Before You Declare Bankruptcy."

National Child Support Enforcement Association
Hall of States
400 N. Capitol St., NW, Suite 372
Washington, DC 20001
202–624–8180
Advises parents on child-support issues.

National College Services
600 S. Frederick Ave.
Gaithersburg, MD 20877
800–662–6275
Provides consultation service regarding financial aid for tuition.

SIX ON THE WEB

www.whitehouse.gov (Welcome to the White House). Admits entry to most government agencies.

www.sbaonline.sba.gov (Small Business Administration). Provides support for the start-up or midlevel entrepreneur.

www.women.com/money (Women.com Networks, Inc.). A full-service personal finance website, written largely by women for women.

www.ed.gov (Department of Education). Includes information about schools and colleges, including financial aid and Hope scholarships.

www.salliemae.com (SallieMae). Contains complete information for the college-bound student, with several calculators to help in planning for tuition.

www.finaid.org (Finaid Page Llc.). A comprehensive review of student financial aid, with information on scholarships and tools by which to calculate the parents' expected contribution.

POCKET MONEY

The ultimate goal of personal finance is to work through all the intricacies and emerge with a simple confidence about money. Keep the problem areas flooded with light, and the same for the dreams and fears that make money important. Know all the basic tools and make use of the strength of proportionality. Work on getting rich, but don't forget to be comfortable and to make sure other people around you will be, too.

In race-car driving, one of the basic lessons is that the best way to steer through a curve is to keep your eyes looking past it, far down the route. With good knowledge, you always know what to do, if you can keep looking down the road.

FURTHER READING

If *EveryDay Money* has introduced personal finance as a game well worth winning (and one that you are already playing, anyway), here are several fine books that cover the subject in bracing detail:

Everybody's Money Book, Jordan E. Goodman and Sonny Block (Dearborn Financial Publishing, 1994).

How to Read the Financial Pages, Peter Passell (New York: Warner Books, 1993).

J. K. Lasser's Your Income Tax, J. K. Lasser Institute (New York: Macmillan, 1994).

Lifetime Book of Money Management, Grace Weinstein (New York: New American Library, 1993).

Personal Financial Planning, G. Victor Hallman and Gerry S. Rosenbloom (New York: McGraw-Hill, 1993).

INDEX